13 Mistresses of Murder

RECOGNITIONS

Mystery Writers

Bruce Cassiday, General Editor

Raymond Chandler by Jerry Speir
P. D. James by Norma Siebenheller
John D. MacDonald by David Geherin
Victorian Masters of Mystery: From Wilkie Collins to Conan Doyle
by Audrey Peterson
Ross Macdonald by Jerry Speir
The Murder Mystique: Crime Writers on Their Art
edited by Lucy Freeman
Roots of Detection: The Art of Deduction before Sherlock Holmes
edited by Bruce Cassiday
Dorothy L. Sayers by Dawson Gaillard
Sons of Sam Spade: The Private Eye Novel in the 70s
by David Geherin
Murder in the Millions: Erle Stanley Gardner—Mickey Spillane—Ian Fleming
by J. Kenneth Van Dover
Rex Stout by David R. Anderson
The American Private Eye: The Image in Fiction
by David Geherin
Dashiell Hammett by Dennis Dooley
The Secret of the Stratemeyer Syndicate: Nancy Drew, the Hardy Boys, and the Million Dollar Fiction Factory
by Carol Billman

13 Mistresses of Murder

Elaine Budd

The Ungar Publishing Company
NEW YORK

Printed in the United States of America.

Library of Congress Cataloging-in-Publication Data

Budd, Elaine.
13 mistresses of murder.

Bibliography: p:
1. Detective and mystery stories, American—Women authors—History and criticism. 2. Detective and mystery stories, English—Women authors—History and criticism. I. Title. II. Title: Thirteen mistresses of murder.
PS374.D4B82 1986 813'.0872'099287 86-1459
ISBN 0-8044-2086-6

Contents

The Oath for Initiation into the Detection Club of London

Dorothy L. Sayers

Do you promise that your detectives shall well and truly detect the crimes presented to them using those wits which it may please you to bestow on them and not placing reliance on nor making use of Divine Revelation, Feminine Intuition, mumbo-jumbo, jiggery-pokery, coincidence or an Act of God?

Do you solemnly swear never to conceal a vital clue from the reader? Do you promise to observe seemly moderation in the use of gangs, conspiracies, Super Criminals and Lunatics and utterly and forever to forswear Mysterious Poisons unknown to science?

Will you honor the King's English?

. . . If you fail to keep your promise, may other writers steal your plots and your pages swarm with misprints.

Introduction
The Second Golden Age Is Here

It's a unique crime, murder, and it arouses strong emotions. Women have always dealt well with the strong emotions.

—P. D. James

There's a new crime wave abroad in the land and it has to do with book sales, not statistics from the blotter of the 17th Precinct. Of the fifteen books listed weekly on the *New York Times* list of best-sellers, as many as seven can be categorized as volumes of mystery or suspense. This hasn't always been true. Since the midnineteenth century, when the first detective story was introduced, public enthusiasm for the genre has waxed and waned, with last rites sometimes performed over the corpse.

The corpse, today, flourishes. Perhaps because mainstream fiction has abdicated its purpose—the telling of a story with a beginning and a middle and an ending. More likely because the best mystery and detective stories have become, simply, some of today's best fiction.

Of these "bests" the writer, today, is quite likely to be a woman. Women, as P. D. James points out, have always dealt well with the strong emotions. In addition they bring to the task of mystery writing traits of patience, wit, tension, and ingenuity. Too, the ability to lie as if telling the truth and telling the truth as if it were a lie is not gender-related but helpful if one happens to be blessed with it.

The thirteen women writers you'll meet here range in age from late thirties to somewhat north of eighty. They reside in cities—New York and London—and in the suburbs of Boston and Los Angeles. One lives in New Mexico; another in a Tudor home in the peaceful Suffolk countryside. One, Lady Antonia Fraser, has a title of the sort that would have warmed the hearts of her spiritual antecedents, Dorothy L. Sayers, Agatha Christie, Ngaio Marsh. One is not "one" at all—but two (Emma Lathen is the pseudonym under which Mary Jane Latsis and Martha Hennisart write). At first glance, they seem to share little in common—except, of course, that each in her own way deals with death. Devilishly. Deliciously.

Although only one of these mistresses of fictional mayhem has, as far as I know, been in the vanguard of the woman's movement (Amanda Cross), each has, consciously or unconsciously, elevated the role of woman, both as role-model writer and in the fictional treatment of woman. Some time ago Dorothy Salisbury Davis wrote, "A woman, to get in on a murder, has to be either dead or deadly, the victim or the murderer." Since those words were written, all manner of female sleuths and protagonists have appeared in detective fiction, most often sprung from the typewriters of women.

There is Jemima Shore, Antonia Fraser's television reporter, a fictional cross between Barbara Walters and Queen Elizabeth I; Davis's own Julie Hayes; and the gutsy ladies who people the works of Dorothy Uhnak and Mary Higgins Clark. There's Amada Cross's Kate Fansler, the feisty, funny Barnard professor who's an ardent feminist, and T. T. Baldwin, Shannon OCork's off-the-wall sports photographer.

"Women are especially good at writing stories about psychological crime," said Mary Higgins Clark during a panel session about women mystery writers at the Third International Crime Congress in Stockholm in 1981. "We have life-enhancing fantasies, and our characters have great warmth and depth to them."

Said P. D. James in a 1981 telephone interview: "Murder is often a domestic matter; that's what makes women good at it. Exploring a killing is a means of discovering the horrific upon peaceful domestic life."

Emotions. Fantasies. Peace and domesticity. Womanly words,

surely. Not the words to describe the works of Dorothy Uhnak, whose fame has come from the bare, brutal crimes involving the police and the politics, the ethnic mix and the social makeup of New York City. Nor Margaret Millar's kooks and kinkies.

Murder, actually, has always been an Equal Opportunity Employer, as Michele Slung points out in her anthology, *Women's Wiles* (Harcourt Brace Jovanovich). Ever since the mystery began to assume a definite shape in the nineteenth century, it has admitted women to all its precincts. As heroine, detective, perpetrator. And as writer.

When Edgar Allan Poe had an errant orangutan stuff a young girl up a chimney in "The Murders in the Rue Morgue" back in 1841 he had no idea then that he'd created a new fiction form — the detective story.

In Victorian England Arthur Conan Doyle took his cue from Poe and augmented his income from a lean medical practice by writing the Sherlock Holmes stories. At the same time on the other side of the Atlantic, Louisa May Alcott fleshed out her own slim royalties from *Little Women* with anonymous chillers such as *Behind the Mask*, and Anna Katharine Green produced *The Leavenworth Case*, the first American best-selling mystery story.

They were followed here at the turn of the century by the prolific Mary Roberts Rinehart, with her intelligent female detective.

The Golden Age of the mystery began after World War I in both England and America. In postwar Britain Dorothy L. Sayers and Agatha Christie and then Margery Allingham and Ngaio Marsh brought their formidable talents to bear on the genre. Sayers's Lord Peter Wimsey, Christie's Poirot, Allingham's Mr. Campion, and Marsh's Rory Alleyn were witty, erudite men who solved upper-class crimes in the sacred clubs and stately homes of England. A bullet creasing a well-tailored dinner jacket, tea gently laced with arsenic in the Spode teapot were the stuff of the English school of crime writing, served up with relish and wry.

In the late 1930s, Dame Daphne du Maurier's *Rebecca* was an international success, while Josephine Tey, an Englishwoman who wrote between the two wars, enjoyed quieter acclaim as a mystery writer for the intelligentsia. Her *A Shilling for Candles* was one of Hitchcock's first films. *The Franchise Affair* was a later movie.

In America, although Raymond Chandler and Dashiell Hammett enjoyed fame, writers such as Dorothy B. Hughes began careers that carry them to the present day. Mrs. Hughes, whose books were made into popular motion pictures in the 1940s, still writes today from her home in New Mexico.

With a deep curtsy to those older writers who continue to spin their webs, my own feeling is that the Golden Age of the mystery for women writers is now, with Clark, Uhnak, James, Ruth Rendell, and others turning out the taut, tight, tense books that appear week after week on the best-seller lists. All write in various subgenres of the mystery and have in common only talent and ingenuity.

One of the mysteries of mystery books is what to call them. Each book doesn't necessarily have a mystery; some don't even have a murder. Methods of presenting plot, character, suspense, atmosphere, problems, and solutions are too wildly different to suggest that one category can cover all these books. In the classic mystery puzzle, the emphasis is on the "thing"—the will, the jewel, the map, or the murder weapon. In a novel of psychological suspense, emphasis is on the characters and what makes them behave as they do. In a romantic suspense tale, emphasis is on the atmosphere—the time, the place, and the influence of both on the characters. In the police procedural, the crime is solved by police through the patient checking of alibis, timetables, and autopsy reports. Stories with an amateur sleuth as protagonist feature the solution of the crime with a dash of charm and a modicum of wit on the part of a detective, who does something else besides chase crooks for a living. A private eye does exactly that: chases crooks for a living.

"My plots come from situations," says Amanda Cross. "I'm not very fond of violence, so what violence there is in my stories I get out of the way fast."

Atmosphere looms large in novels of romantic suspense. "My books begin with a unique place, its color and its ambience," says Phyllis Whitney. "I begin there, try to find the right mix of people to put in that place." Lucy Freeman is involved in the "whydunit" rather than the "whodunit" of a crime, the psychological mainsprings from which a crime evolves.

The three Englishwomen you'll meet here—Ruth Rendell, P. D. James, and Antonia Fraser—are lavish with detail and are not in the least cozy.

James, who admits to being influenced by Sayers and Allingham, both of whom had attractive male detectives, introduced Inspector Adam Dalgliesh of New Scotland Yard in her first book, *Cover Her Face* (1961), written while the author held down a full-time job. James's other detective, Cordelia Gray, a snappy young female sleuth, appeared first in *An Unsuitable Job for a Woman.*

Jemima Shore is the brainchild of Lady Antonia Fraser, previously known in literary circles for her biographies and histories. Member of a titled English Catholic family, Lady Antonia placed Jemima's first caper, *Quiet as a Nun*, in a convent school much like the one Lady Antonia attended in her youth.

"Ruth Rendell is a very evil lady," commented one mystery book club editor. Rendell has, at various times, had a child disappear down a well, invited wasps to a birthday party, inflicted an eye hemorrhage on a chief inspector. Not exactly the lady to be read by someone planning to settle down with a quiet comfortable tea-and-strychnine novel for an hour or two.

I have interviewed almost all of the women in this book, either in person or by telephone and in some cases by both methods. I was gratified to discover how interested the women writers were in each other. "Oh, *what's* she like?" Clark asked me about Fraser. Clark was especially intrigued by a writer like herself, and her age, writing from as thorough a grounding in the Roman Catholic church as Clark herself does.

To Clark I could truthfully answer: "She is bright and beautiful and funny and very much at home with herself. As you are."

As indeed they all are. The entire devious, devilish, delicious baker's dozen of them!

Elaine Budd
East Haddam, Connecticut

1

Mary Higgins Clark

Menace of the Innocents

What if . . . someone such as Alice Crimmins (the New York cocktail waitress who was convicted of killing her small son) went to prison, served her time, was released, remarried, had other children . . . *and it all happened again*? That's the sort of "what ifs" Mary Higgins Clark asks herself, and the answers produce some of today's most electrifying suspense novels.

That "what if" was the basis of the plot of Clark's first suspense novel, *Where Are the Children?* The fact that readers can almost—but not quite—identify a behind-the-headlines element in her books may account partially for their success. The menace of innocents is a recurring theme for Clark—a theme that has gripped readers since the days of Hansel and Gretel.

Clark has been writing for almost thirty years. "My first short story was sent out forty times before it finally sold to *Extension Magazine* for a hundred dollars. How's that for persistence?"

Now in her early fifties, Clark grew up in the Bronx, New York, the daughter of the owner of a New York restaurant-bar. Her mother was a buyer for a New York department store. As a child Clark suffered from asthma and spent many years propped up among her pillows listening to the radio.

"I didn't go to college after I graduated from high school," she says. "I was an airline stewardess. I traveled all over the world for a year before I married Warren Clark.

"Then I went to work in an advertising agency and I knew I *had* to learn to write. We lived in New York's Stuyvesant Town, an apartment complex filled with other young marrieds. I enrolled in a writing course at New York University. The professor in that course said, 'If you have a unique background, *write* it.' It was good advice. I used my stewardess background in that first short story.

"I still meet weekly with some of the members of that NYU class, because I find the discipline of writing with, and for, a group tremendously stimulating."

Clark's first writing success turned out to be a more personal coup than a short story. She wrote about it in the 1982 issue of the *Mystery Writers' Annual*.

"In the spring of 1955, I was on line in the bakery in Manhattan. I was holding in my hand the envelope bearing the latest rejected manuscript. My three children were crawling all over me; I was scarcely aware of them. This time the editor had gone out of her way to turn the knife. On the printed rejection slip she'd scrawled, 'Your stories are light, slight, and trite.'

"Would I ever make it as a writer? Was I kidding myself by trying?

"On the wall a poster announced a contest the bakery was conducting. Four designer dresses were sketched on the poster: a Chanel, a Dior, a Givenchy, and a Norell. In twenty-five words or less the contestants were instructed to complete the following sentence: 'I choose the (name of designer) creation because. . . .'

"The Givenchy was a lovely thing. Typical of the fifties, it had layers of swirling black silk, layers of crinoline, puffed sleeves, and a tiny waist. I fell in love with it. The sales clerk held the blank steady as I wrote:

> I choose the Givenchy creation because I have three young children and it's a long time since I've felt irresistible. I am sure that in that gown I could feel irresistible plus.

"I won the contest and for years wore the Givenchy for all Grand Occasions. To me it was more than a dress. It was visible evidence that maybe I had, as my mother put it, a 'way with words' and could break into writing."

After forty submissions, Clark's short story sold, and she began to believe that she could, indeed, write. The story did well from a critical view and has been anthologized.

Clark was only thirty-four years old when her husband died of a heart attack in 1964. With five children now, aged from five to thirteen, she began commuting from her suburban home in New Jersey to Manhattan where she wrote copy for radio broadcasts. She did four-minute scripts for "Portrait of a Patriot," a five-a-week radio show hosted by Bud Collier. She also turned out radio scripts for Bess Myerson's food show and Hugh Downs's driving-home show. She wondered if she could sustain a full-length book.

The book that resulted was a biography of George Washington, which grew out of one of her radio scripts.

"*Aspire to the Heavens* is a collector's item today," says Clark of the volume. "The print order was for seventeen hundred copies. Most went to my relatives. The bookstores thought it was a prayer book and put it in the religious section.

"When I began writing *Where Are the Children?* I got up at 5 A.M. every morning so that I could put in an hour or two on the book before going to work. You don't put off writing."

Where Are the Children? was rejected by two publishers before Simon & Schuster bought it for an advance of three thousand dollars.

"At that time I had two children in law school, one at Dartmouth, one at Mt. Holyoke, and one in private school. I looked at the tuition bills and just about decided it was second-mortgage time —I had already hocked everything there was to hock—when my agent phoned to say that Dell had bought the paperback rights for one hundred thousand dollars! I gave the biggest party!

"It was the most enormous weight off my shoulders. Of course, Simon & Schuster received 50 percent of the money and the taxes on the remaining 50 percent were mind-boggling. But it meant that all the children could go back to school without worrying over tuition or loans or having to work.

"I couldn't afford to quit my radio job, however, until *A Stranger Is Watching* sold to Simon & Schuster for a half million dollars and the paperback rights sold for a million dollars."

Not only could Clark pay the tuition for all the children, but now she could afford to go to college herself. She graduated summa cum laude from Fordham University in 1979 with a bachelor's degree in philosophy. To celebrate, Clark threw a senior prom—the one she would have had in 1949 if she had graduated from college four years after her graduation from high school.

With homes in New Jersey, Cape Cod, and an apartment in New York City, she is in business with two of her children, producing radio shows. Her books have been translated into many foreign languages. In 1980 she was awarded the French Grand Prix Policier (France's equivalent of the Mystery Writers of America's Edgar) for *Where Are the Children?*

Clark is a master storyteller who builds her taut suspense stories in a limited time frame. *Where Are the Children?* begins at 9 A.M. and ends at 7 P.M. the same day. Only three days elapse in *A Stranger Is Watching*.

"I believe in containment," Clark explained in an interview in the *Washington Post* in 1980. "I like something I can control. It's like Oedipus Rex saying: 'It's a lousy day. My wife committed suicide, I'm blinded, and the kingdom is going to pot.'"

A Stranger Is Watching was made into a motion picture released in 1982. *The Cradle Will Fall* became a television movie in the summer of 1983.

Where Are the Children? has been made into a motion picture with Jill Clayburgh, and is currently (1986) in release. Actress Lynda Carter has bought *Stillwatch* as a starring vehicle for herself. And Clark recently collaborated with mystery writers Gregory MacDonald and Robert Parker on a mini-mystery for the television show *Good Morning, America*. "We wrote it in one day," she says of the project. *Weep No More, My Lady*, her latest book, is scheduled for late 1986 release from Simon & Schuster.

Clark feels strongly that men should write about men and women should write about women. "I don't think that a man could have written *Jane Eyre* or that a woman could have written *Treasure Island* at the time those books were written. Even when I took my first writing course, the professor said, 'Men should write about men and women about women.' I gulped and thought about Agatha Christie and Charlotte Armstrong, who wrote equally well from a woman's or a man's point of view.

"Women do tend to be offstage: a cloud passes over the moon when someone is about to be murdered. But we write what we must write, and we bring a special ingredient of warmth and understanding to our characters. We are sensitive: we perceive emotional situations before men do.

"The 'Perils of Pauline' is over, however. We no longer wait for men to rescue us. Today a woman protagonist wouldn't run to a man for help. If her children are missing, she'll go for the children herself.

"I like to write about very nice people who are confronted by the forces of evil and who, through their own intelligence, work their way through to deliverance," said Clark in an interview in *Twin Cities Magazine* in September 1982.

Clark's stories are of the quiet terror lurking beneath the surface of an ordinary life. "I write about people not looking for trouble. They find evil in their own car, their home, their everyday life."

Even though the spark of the idea for *Where Are the Children?* came from the Alice Crimmins case, the novel does not parallel the case.

"I just thought of a mother of children who had been murdered who is then tried for their murders," she says, "and took the next step to the possible."

Where Are the Children?

Seven years before the novel begins, California police did not really believe Nancy Harmon's pleas of innocence in the gruesome deaths of her two children, Peter and Lisa, whose bodies were found washed up from the ocean with plastic bags tied over their heads. The district attorney did not believe in her innocence either. Nancy's husband, Professor Carl Harmon, did not believe in her, and subsequently committed suicide by drowning, after almost accusing Nancy of the tragedy on the witness stand. The jury would have found her guilty had not a legal technicality saved her. Rob Legler, a student of Carl's who once tried to make love to Nancy and who testified against her, deserted from the army, fled across the border to Canada, and disappeared rather than face service in Vietnam.

Forced to release Nancy, the district attorney swore he'd bring her to trial again when Legler was found.

Released from jail, Nancy fled across the country. She cut and dyed brown her notorious and recognizable red hair. She rebuilt her life in Adams Port, a small town on Cape Cod. Married to Ray Eldredge, the young real estate man who rented her the small cottage, Nancy now has—again—two young children, Michael and Missy.

As the novel opens, it is seven o'clock in the morning of a blustery fall day. Ray Eldredge comes into the kitchen, where Nancy holds a sleepy Missy, and watches Michael eating his breakfast. He kisses his wife.

"Happy birthday, honey." He feels her tremble at the words. It's time, the words say. Time to forget the past—and that other birthday seven years ago, when her first children died. Michael and Missy are excited about the birthday. They'll invite Aunt Dorothy for dinner that night, have a party. Dorothy, an older woman who works with Ray, is the only other person on the Cape who knows Nancy's true identity.

But it is not destined to be a happy birthday.

Ray goes to work. Nancy dresses the children for the outdoors, putting on jackets, pulling red mittens over Missy's hands, fighting the normal terror she always feels at letting her children out of her sight. They go out to their swing. Nancy brings in the weekly Cape Cod newspaper, fixes herself a cup of coffee, turning the pages.

"No! No! No!" The coffee is spilled as Nancy cries out in pain and in panic. *Can This Be a Happy Birthday for Nancy Harmon?* screams the headline of a story in the paper, which goes on to say: "Somewhere today Nancy Harmon is celebrating her thirty-second birthday and the seventh anniversary of the death of the children she was found guilty of murdering." The story contains photographs: one of Carl and Rob Legler leaving the trial; another of Nancy and Peter and Lisa; and a third, newly taken, showing Nancy as she is today. The latter would alert everyone on Cape Cod to the fact that Nancy Harmon was now Nancy Eldredge!

In panic, Nancy burns the newspaper in the fireplace, and runs to the door, calling the children.

But the children are not there. The swing where Michael has been pushing Missy sways gently in the wind; a small red mitten is caught on it.

Nancy runs outside, calling. Fighting rising panic, she runs down to the lake on the property. Something shimmers beneath the surface of the lake and she plunges into the icy waters. The shimmer turns out to be nothing. Exhausted, Nancy pulls herself up on the frozen bank and sees in the woods the face of a man, somehow familiar, just before she loses consciousness.

In icy counterpoint to the warmth of the Eldredge family and home, the reader sees Courtenay Parrish, a mysterious, hulking figure who, yearly, rents the third-floor apartment of an ancient, ruined mansion overlooking the bay, across the water from the Eldredge home. He has a large telescope trained on the Eldredge dwelling, where he watches every move. He shakes with mirth at the surprises he has in store for Nancy. First the article in the newspaper; that will turn her comfortable life upside down! He checks his pockets. The needles are there, filled, ready to produce instant sleep. Perspiration starts down his arms as he lumbers down the stairs into the station wagon. A canvas coat lies ready to cover the children's bodies. Ten minutes of ten.

He drives along the road backing the Eldredge property. It is but the work of a few minutes as he gives quick jabs with the needles first to the boy, then to the tiny girl. At five minutes of ten they lie crumpled under the canvas coat. Courtenay doesn't notice that one small mitten is left caught on the children's swing. At four minutes after ten he walks into Wiggins Market, buys a quart of milk and leaves.

Back in the apartment, he feels a thrill of satisfaction. He throws the unconscious children on the bed. When the little girl awakens, Courtenay plans to give her a bath, dry her off with a soft towel, rub baby powder all over her, kiss her. A sob tells him one child is awake.

"I want to go home," says the boy.

"You can't go home. Look there, through the telescope." There is the burst of activity. Police cars coming and going, the lake being churned by a diver. "I'm supposed to watch you. Your mommy went to God this morning."

"If Mommy went to God, then I want to go, too!"

The man smiles. "You will. Tonight. I promise you."

Jonathan Knowles is a retired lawyer now living in Adams Port. He is working on a book called *Verdict in Doubt*, about ten controversial cases; he has hired a free-lance researcher to put together files on each case. He will soon begin the chapter devoted to the Nancy Harmon case. He pulls out the research, clippings and files, but before he begins to work, he opens the Cape Cod newspaper and discovers that what he has suspected all along—that Nancy Eldredge is in reality Nancy Harmon—is true. And, regretfully, he realizes that Dorothy, Ray's assistant, has lied to him; she has told Jonathan that she knew Nancy's family back in Virginia.

Jed Coffin, the Adams Port police chief, is called in. Chagrined that he hasn't recognized Nancy Eldredge as Nancy Harmon, he believes that the woman has gone berserk after seeing the article in the Cape Cod newspaper and has killed Michael and Missy. He tries to talk to Nancy, who has been found by the pond and brought home, to get her to tell him where the children are. But it is useless. She is barely conscious; she can't tell Jed anything. The officer launches a full-scale search for the children and the story is released to the news media.

In Boston, Dr. Lendon Miles, psychiatrist, hears the news on the radio as he begins lunch at his desk; hears it with a shadow of pain. Nancy's mother, a widow, was working for Miles when Nancy began college in California. He realized he was in love with Priscilla when he put her on the plane to California to visit her daughter. Priscilla never returned. She was killed when her rental car went out of control. Miles was concerned for Priscilla's daughter Nancy; when he phoned, however, Nancy was at the home of one of her professors—Carl Harmon—and plans were hastened for their marriage. So Miles closed the book on that chapter of his life and went off to England. When he returned, Nancy was on trial for the murder of her children. He always wondered where Nancy vanished to after she was freed.

Now he knows. She's been living only an hour away. Maybe he can make up for having failed her before. He cancels his four o'clock class, picks up his raincoat and heads for Adams Port.

Someone else has arrived in Adams Port. Rob Legler, the "other man" in the Harmon case and a sort of counter-culture celebrity living in a Canadian hideaway, has been told by a friend that Nancy Harmon is living on Cape Cod; in fact, a Polaroid snapshot sent to him proves it. Knowing it is time to cash in on the past, Rob drives his red Dodge to Adams Port, telling a gas station attendant that he's going to a place where "They won't be happy to see me." He passes an old station wagon as he skirts the Eldredge property and prepares to visit Nancy Eldredge to collect for keeping his mouth shut.

Though Jed Coffin wants to take Nancy to police headquarters to question her, Ray persuades him to leave the stricken woman at home. Lendon Miles and Jonathan Knowles arrive at the same time, as does Dorothy. Knowles, after reading his notes about the Harmon case, and realizing that Nancy should never have taken the stand in her own defense, offers to represent her. Miles wants to hypnotize Nancy to get at the truth of what happened seven years ago and thus perhaps gain some insight into where the Eldredge children are. The chief of police reluctantly allows him to do this.

Dorothy, Ray's assistant, leaves the Eldredge home to take a real estate client from New York – John Kragopoulos – to see the old Hill mansion, where Courtenay Parrish is renting. The client hopes to turn the building into a restaurant. Dorothy is upset and explains to Kragopoulos about the Eldredge children. The two inspect the old mansion, arriving at the third-floor apartment to find a visibly upset Parrish. Kragopoulos is disgusted upon opening the door to the bathroom to see that Parrish has drawn a tub for a bath, with a rubber duck floating in the water! As the two leave, Dorothy sees a small red mitten in the garage – a mitten that must have fallen from her car. She had taken the two Eldredge children out with her yesterday, buying them ice cream cones, and Missy must have left the mitten there.

She takes Kragopoulos back to her office, apologizes for leaving him to get back to the house and rushes back to the Cape. Kragopoulos leaves for New York.

The remainder of the book is a breathtaking race to see if the doctor can unlock Nancy's subconscious before Courtenay Parrish (who is Nancy's unbalanced pedophiliac first husband) can molest and then kill Michael and Missy.

Driving to New York, Kragopoulos muses about the rubber duck he has seen in Parrish's apartment, and, remembering the red mitten that Dorothy has picked up, stops his car and turns it around. He takes his gold lighter from his pocket, puts it in the glove compartment, and heads back to the Hill mansion.

At one point in the action young Michael escapes long enough from his captor to phone home. Only Nancy and Dorothy are there. Before Michael can say where he and Missy are, the phone goes dead. It is Nancy who puzzles out where her son must be, and it is Nancy who goes out to get her children.

Clark's narrative moves along in a mass of swiftly successive scenes against the stark backdrop of a blustery Cape Cod day. It is the author's experience in writing for radio, perhaps, that explains the lithe lines of her story. In radio, the writer has only dialogue and sound effects with which to delineate character, evolve plot, move action and bring resolution. It is a spare, lean, and above all active voice—radio—and Clark uses her experience with it surely and deftly in the suspense genre.

"During the writing of this book," said Clark, "I didn't know, at one point, if Nancy's husband—Ray—ought to have a moment of doubt about whether or not his wife could possibly have done something with their children, given her history. I was honestly puzzled. That's where my creative writing group turned out to be invaluable. Said one member: 'If Ray has one second of doubt about Nancy—ever—then this book doesn't work.' Of course she was right. I'd become so immersed in my story I'd momentarily lost track of what my characters were about."

Clark's heroines are today's women—assertive without being aggressive. The religious faith of her Gaelic forefathers and mothers, as well as their wit, shines through her writing.

Says Dr. Albert Silverstein, professor of psychology at the University of Rhode Island and a mystery buff (he is the Chaldean Archivist of the Cornish Horrors scion of the Baker Street Irregulars society), "Mystery stories are so popular because they provide a context in which mysterious and puzzling events come out in a clear way. All parents worry about the safety of their children." Clark vents the fear; it all stops in the nick of time. Everything comes out all right.

One learns about the character of the actors in the drama by their words and their actions. The major plot line is skillfully interwoven—braided, perhaps, is a better word—with several subplots so tightly and tautly that they evolve all of a piece.

"Sometimes I've believed as many as six impossible things before breakfast," said the Queen to Alice in *Through the Looking Glass*. If there is a cavil at all to Clark's book, it's that there are one or two suggestions the reader is asked to believe that stretch credulity. The first is that the suicide of Nancy's first husband is presented to us as a fact that happened; that Carl drowned himself. It seems unlikely that an aroused citizenry and a headline-grabbing DA accepted the fact of this suicide without further investigation or search for a body. A second point: would a careful murderer have been so careless as to let drop from the hands of his victim *two* bright red mittens—the first in her yard and the second in his garage—Hansel-and-Gretel clues that could lead directly to him? And Rob Legler's Canadian friend, spotting Nancy Harmon-Eldredge on Cape Cod, has to be considered as one of those rare needle-in-a-haystack coincidences that must be almost impossible to believe.

But that is to quibble. The pace of the narrative, the skillful limning of character in spare action rather than in paragraphs of description, the skill of the plot point to the debut of an exciting storyteller at the very beginning of the exploration of her gifts. The quiet agony of a family suddenly exploded by menace is a universal theme. The presentation to Clark of the French Grand Prix Policier for the book indicates that readers the world over identify with it.

Perhaps the main difference between Clark and her male counterpart detective writers is that Clark's books are rationally softened. In many successful stories written by men there are scenes of sex, of violence. In Clark's books there are honest feelings—of warmth, of love. Readers do not find explicit sex in these books. As in radio, a lot is left to the imagination. Gory details happen off camera. Her plots hook the reader, nevertheless.

"The first thing I am is a storyteller," says Clark. "All the beautiful writing in the world doesn't matter if the story doesn't grab the reader."

2

Amanda Cross

In the Groves of Academe

Amanda Cross is the pseudonym of Carolyn Heilbrun of New York City, a professor of Modern English Literature at Columbia University. Heilbrun is a prolific writer in her own field of literature, as well as in the field of feminist writing (she was an early and ardent supporter of the woman's movement) and has chosen to write her mystery books featuring Kate Fansler under the Cross name.

"I grew up in New York City, went to Wellesley, got a Ph.D. in literature at Columbia, and I teach there now. I've been teaching at Columbia since 1960, and I have been a full professor at the university since 1972. They took a long time to promote women in those days." Heilbrun is in her early fifties.

"Shades of Kate Fansler." She laughs. Fansler is Cross's feisty detective protagonist, who is a Barnard professor and a feminist. "You can write that if you want to," she says, "but I won't admit it. Kate is a fantasy as is any character in detective fiction—or at any rate, an artifact."

Heilbrun-Cross was born and grew up in New York City, not far from where she now lives on the city's West Side. "I didn't come from a family of writers, but I came from a family of readers, which is almost as important. I can remember when I was very young my mother reading Virginia Woolf and Henry James."

Heilbrun is married to James Heilbrun, an economist. They live close to Lincoln Center, and have two subscriptions to the ballets housed therein. They have a summer home in the Massachusetts Berkshires (and where *The James Joyce Murders* takes place). The Heilbruns have two daughters, a son, and a cat. The oldest daughter is a lawyer. The two younger Heilbrun children are twins, a boy and a girl. The boy is in law school; the girl is an artist.

"It's wonderful having grown-up children. They now read the books before I publish them and they find all the mistakes that I've made. They are very intelligent and entertaining and generally we feel very blessed."

Heilbrun's favorite mystery writers are "all the great ones from the Golden Years—Sayers, especially. Some of them are still writing: Michael Gilbert, for one. My own field of expertise is Modern British Literature, from the 1870s until World War II.

"My affection and admiration for Michael Gilbert are not hard to understand: He is a member of a generation of men whose works I regularly teach and learn about in the field of modern British literature. Born in those years of this century that preceded World War I, they were young men in the thirties and were of an age—on the old side in some cases—to take part in World War II."[1]

Heilbrun has written extensively in her own field of expertise, as well as in the field of feminism. Of *Reinventing Womanhood*, one of her books in the latter field, she writes, "I have taught a lot of courses about feminist literature and I have been very outspoken on the whole women's movement, very involved in it and interested in it."

Ten years ago Heilbrun published the book *Toward a Recognition of Androgyny*, about the male-female principle in each of us. "I thought of Viola and Sebastian, the girl-boy twins in Shakespeare's *Twelfth Night* and of course I have girl-boy twins. I now feel different about the subject. That's the interesting thing. I keep growing and people ask me about books I wrote before and it's as if a different person wrote the book than the one who's contemplating it at the present."

In the midsixties, during all the turmoil of the feminist movement, Heilbrun wrote her first Kate Fansler mystery. The heroine is a spunky lady professor with an impeccable Back Bay background and money, a professor at Barnard College. Given Heilbrun's admiration for Dorothy L. Sayers, one can almost see Kate Fansler as a modern-day Harriet Vane (Sayers's lady detective, who taught at Oxford, later married to Lord Peter Wimsey).

Heilbrun got up early in the morning to write her first Fansler book. "I'm one of these people who only gets something done if I'm busy. Given all day to accomplish something, I seem to be able to do—nothing." It takes her about three years to write each Fansler mystery, given her hectic teaching and writing schedule.

The books, each with a university ambience, generally have as leitmotif the works of one of the major writers that are Cross-Heilbrun's speciality: James Joyce, or Auden, or T. S. Eliot.

"I tend to write what I call the 'English Cozy' type of story, where a lot of people sit around talking. I'm not very fond of violence, so what violence there is in my stories I get out of the way very fast."

Plots? They mostly come from themes, or situations. "What if this happened, then what would so and so do?" Since the books are set in a university background, the "what ifs" often come from such amiable university questions as "Will Professor Windworthy, instructor in Greek Classics, be granted tenure?"

"Murder doesn't have to be a dreadful, dreary business. It can be told in a civilized, witty, and learned fashion with an observant eye on society's pretentions and pomposities. And no one has a sharper eye than Amanda Cross, whose delightful Kate Fansler, professor-cum-sleuth, returns to find *Death in a Tenured Position.*"[2]

Cross has the sharp eye of a Jane Austen and the wit of a Rex Stout, an author whom she admires. "I don't like the tough Hammett-Chandler school of writing. It's not my universe. I don't agree with Chandler that you have to write about people to whom murder is an everyday occurrence. I think the entire point of detective fiction is that it occurs where murder is possible because human beings are present. But I don't feel it is an everyday occurrence."

Latest Fansler book (appearing in spring 1984) is *Sweet Death, Kind Death*, which is a quote from British poet Stevie Smith.

Professor Heilbrun's major gripe about her university position is one basic to the entire woman's movement—the fact that women professors are paid less than men.

"No question women get paid less. Still do. We had a thing at Columbia, and we had a committee look at all the salaries and some adjusting was done. But we had all started at so much lower salaries than men that I and my outstanding women colleagues are still paid less. The only way to redress that particular grievance is to take another job. I have been offered other jobs, but I don't want to leave New York City. I'm an incurable New Yorker."

Death in a Tenured Position

"I frankly don't *care* whodunit," says Carol Brener, owner of Murder Ink, the mystery bookshop in New York City. "I read a mystery for everything else: the cozy, or haunting, or evil environment, and the extraordinary people who inhabit it."

There must be many readers out there like Brener. According to a Gallup Survey, mystery novels outsold all other fiction categories in 1983.

And in an unofficial survey of one—me—of the Idontcarewhodunit writers, the best is Amanda Cross and the Kate Fansler books. The fact is that in the Fansler books, Cross gets her murders and her bodies out of the way fast. There is not really a lot of effective police work done in a Cross novel nor are there many clues found and followed up.

When I reread *Death in a Tenured Position* for discussion here, I found that I remembered neither who the victim was nor who it was who did her in. On the other hand, the book is eminently rereadable, being filled with the sort of witty, literate chitchat that one would expect to hear in the commons room of the faculty of a smart, bright institution of learning. Literary allusions fly—and not necessarily the best-known ones. I should imagine that Heilbrun is a fine lecturer.

The murders and murderers/murderesses are quite beside the point in a Cross book.

And the police, when alluded to at all, are placed on a back burner, while Kate, with a sometime assist from her long-playing and long-suffering fiancé (later husband) Reed Amhearst, district attorney, knits up the skeins of story lines and solves the crime with a certain élan.

There are several story lines in *Death in a Tenured Position*.

The first: an unknown benefactor has endowed a professorial chair in the English department of Harvard University for a million dollars, with the stipulation that the chair be filled by a woman professor. The offer sets the cat among the pigeons: Harvard, and especially the English department, has given lip service to the quality of women professors (while admitting that it is the women who are getting the high marks as students), but never done much more than talk about the subject.

After a search, Professor Janet Mandelbaum is selected for the position, and scarcely has she got settled into Cambridge than a scandal erupts. It seems that she has gotten tipsy at a faculty party, gone into the women's bathroom of the English Department house, and fallen into the bathtub. When found, a woman who's a member of a notorious local commune of lesbians is discovered in the tub with Janet. Sensation!

Kate's help is enlisted by a friend who is, like Kate, an ardent feminist (though Professor Mandelbaum herself is not one). Still, Kate and Sylvia, a member of the Washington Old Girl network, can see the absurdities of the over-ardent commune feminists, who completely abjure the world of men even as they regret the attitude of Janet Mandelbaum, who feels that "if I can make it in a man's world, so can everyone else." Kate can smile when she spots an inscription on the mirror in a women's room: "Trust in God; She will provide."

Kate takes leave from her Barnard position and goes to Cambridge as a member of visiting faculty at Radcliffe. Before the end of her stay she will have to deliver one lecture to the resident Cliffies. Most of her time, however, is free, so she wanders the town of Cambridge, the Harvard campus. Kate's niece, Leighton, a thoroughly refreshing member of the Harvard junior class, is on hand. So are some of Kate's old friends, among who is Professor Milton (called "Moon") Mandelbaum, on leave from the University of Minnesota, where he is in charge of the writing program, and teaching this term at Harvard. He taught Kate and Janet when both were grad students, was a favorite professor of both, and married Janet. The marriage did not last.

Head of the English department is Dr. Clarkville, tradition-bound, homosexual, unfriendly to the entire idea of Janet Mandelbaum and her professorship. Before Kate leaves for Harvard, Mark Evergreen, a colleague at the Faculty Club at Columbia, describes Clarkville to her.

> "Of course," Mark added, "he's gay. But you know that."
>
> "So I have heard," Kate said. "Lively, merry, and given to the wearing of bright colors; full of sprightly activity."
>
> "Oh, dear," Mark said. "I ought not to have mentioned it so flatly. You are offended."
>
> "Only by the word. I mourn for words. Clarissa Dalloway thought of Peter Walsh, 'If I had married him this gaiety would have been mine all day.' Could one write that sentence now? It would evoke the kind of snicker reminiscent of those occasions in my childhood when one innocently referred to fairies. Perhaps, if gay comes to mean homosexual, we shall recover fairies to describe the wee folk, living at the bottom of my garden, or anywhere else."

Not long after Kate's arrival in Cambridge, Janet Mandelbaum is discovered sitting up in one of the stalls of the men's room of the English building—dead from cyanide poisoning.

The police, after a certain amount of investigation, arrest Moon Mandelbaum, Janet's ex-husband, as her murderer. It turns out that he has kept a cache of cyanide at home in his attic since World War II. Moon uses his one telephone call to summon Kate to his side. She brings with her a lawyer, who's a member of the Boston establishment and an old friend of hers and Reed's.

Kate embarks on a number of ploys right out of the "English Cozy" world of detectives, including the gathering all the suspects in one room for a party so she can cross-examine them. She then rather conveniently examines the dead professor's digs in Cambridge, the professor's office at Harvard, and eventually comes up with the answer to Mandelbaum's death, from a volume of seventeenth-century poetry found open on Janet's desk.

And that's it! End of mystery, taking up as little time as possible in a book filled with acerbic wit, delicious comedy and marvelous characters (including a dog named Jocasta, who has an eccentric personality and an extremely catholic diet).

Police work and police themselves are given very short shrift in the book, there being more wit and charm in the Kate Fansler books than there is mystery and detection. This lack apparently does not bother the powers-that-be in the mystery field. Ms. Cross's first Fansler book, *In the Last Analysis*, received a scroll from the Mystery Writers of America as one of the best first novels of its year, and *Death in a Tenured Position* received the 1981 Nero Wolfe award for mystery fiction.

I want to quote one more item, written by Heilbrun herself (in a *Washington Post Book World* review of *A Coat of Varnish*, C. P. Snow's 1971 mystery, written when the gentleman was in his seventies):

"But don't read it for the plot, or else, as Samuel Johnson said in another connection, you may hang yourself. And if you do, please leave a note saying who did it. Murder stories must have an orderly ending. It may be the only order we've got left."[3]

Cross's Fansler stories do have orderly endings. They generally have sprightly beginnings, as well. It is the solutions that sometimes suggest more sleight-of-hand than productive hard-won detective work. Still, as Carol Brener said earlier, "I don't care whodunit; I read a book for everything else." The Fansler books can surely be read for everything else.

3

Dorothy Salisbury Davis

Mysteries within Mysteries

"If she's very lucky, a writer will sometimes receive a gift. I've had a couple of gifts in my lifetime. *A Gentle Murderer* was one. A gift from God, if you will. It came so easily, that book. It went so beautifully and so straight and so *right* from the beginning. I knew the first sentence was to be 'Bless me, Father, for I have sinned,' and that's how it went, all the way through. It was my third book, published back in 1951, and it's since been republished four times."

That's Dorothy Salisbury Davis speaking, a writer's writer, admired by her peers and by the critics and perhaps not as well known among the general reading public as she should be. Newgate Calendar once noted that the genre became for her a vehicle for the development of character.[1]

Davis has won seven scrolls from the Mystery Writers of America (a scroll is the runner-up award to an Edgar) but has never won an Edgar. "I don't suppose I'd trade the scrolls in for one Edgar," Davis said recently in a magazine interview. "But I might. The stunning commentary is that I'm the kid who always wanted to be first in the class."[2]

(The kid who always wanted to be first is now an adult with short gray hair, enormous energy, and a great good humor who helps guide the Mystery Writers of America from her place on its board. At the 1985 MWA Edgar Awards Dinner, Davis received its highest honor: that of Grand Master.)

Crises of faith, sexual conflicts, and identity problems are what Davis writes about, "and I've used them to the bottom of the cup. I escaped into escape. I have not escaped, of course."[3]

Nevertheless, her love/hate relationship with the Roman Catholic Church, and the fact that she was an adopted child, account for the exploration throughout her works of articles of faith, of commitment, and of the search for one's roots, which give her readers more than the one-dimensional look of many standard mystery books.

Born in Chicago, Illinois, on April 26, 1916, Dorothy Salisbury Davis was adopted by Margaret Jane and Alfred Joseph Salisbury. Her mother was a North-of-Ireland Catholic, who didn't leave Ireland until she was twenty-seven years old. Her father was born in Dorset, England, and came to this country at the age of seven.

"He loved the Army," Davis said in the *EQMM* interview. "He fought in the Spanish-American War, the Philippine Insurrection and in World War I. A convert to the Catholic Church, he was far more religious than my mother."[4]

When the author was five, her father left his job in the steel mills to buy a farm. It was a life he loved (as did Dorothy) and one that her mother hated. While young Dorothy got up at five in the morning to help her father with the farm chores ("In those early days I'd have to say he won the perpetual struggle between them for my allegiance"[5]) it was her mother who shared the music and the books and the movies with the girl that were her mother's solace, and in the end it was her reclusive mother who stepped out and bargained for the scholarship that would send Dorothy to college.

"Her imagination enriched my childhood," remembers Davis in the *EQMM* interview. "And her language, with its depth of Irish lore. When I was hopeless, she'd say, 'My heart's scalded with you.' To the question, 'What's for supper?' she'd answer, 'Sweeps heels and roasted snow.'"

At seventeen, quite by accident, Davis discovered she was adopted. "The floor tilted half over and then settled into place again." It was over a year later that she confessed to her parents that she knew she was adopted.

Davis graduated from Barat College in 1938, at the tag end of the Depression. She spent the next year promoting Keystone the

Magician on the road, in towns of from ten to thirty thousand population, one a week, throughout the Northeast and the Midwest. "Lonely as an owl and often hungry, I found in every human contact a little of the ecstasy of first love."[6]

A more satisfying love developed a few years later, when on a blind date in Chicago Dorothy was introduced to Harry Davis, an actor in the city with the Broadway company of the show *Jacobowski and the Colonel*. They were married in 1946. The Davises make their permanent home in Sneden's Landing, Palisades, New York. They have no children.

Davis's first novel, *The Judas Cat*, was set in a small midwestern town and concerns a young newspaper publisher's inquiry into the death of a reclusive old man. The author's next book, *The Clay Hand*, also reaches into the past as a sheriff looks into the death of an investigative reporter who intrudes upon a West Virginia mining town. Her third book—Davis's personal favorite—was *A Gentle Murderer*.

From the first, Davis's books have been published by Charles Scribners' Sons. "I've been with Scribners longer than any other living writer. They give me a good home. My long-time editor at Scribners, Burroughs Mitchell, was responsible for our move to Rockland County," Davis told me.

Throughout the fifties, Davis produced almost a mystery novel a year, alternating in background between her native Midwest and her new home, New York. She next devoted herself to two novels outside the mystery field. *Men of No Property* is about the coming of the Irish to New York in the midnineteenth century, while *The Evening of the Good Samaritan* is a novel of generations in a large midwestern city. With two exceptions (*Enemy and Brother* is a novel of intrigue in Greece based on the still-unsolved murder of CBS correspondent George L. Polk during the Greek Civil War, and *God Speed the Night*, written in collaboration with Jerome Ross, the story of a nun's heroism and sacrifice in occupied France during World War II) her novels to date shift back and forth from the same settings.

Davis once wrote, "A woman, to get in on a murder, has to be either dead or deadly, the victim or the murderer."[7] Since she wrote that, and indeed since the advent of the woman's movement, there has been a strong flow of women detectives to join the mainstream of mystery fiction. Davis's contribution to the gaggle of distaff sleuths is Julie Hayes, housewife, reader, and advisor, who becomes involved in crime investigation in *A Death in the Life*, written in 1976.

"I wanted to have some fun," Davis told me. "I wanted to break a writing block, and to break the block the only way I could was simple—to have fun. In doing so, I did something terrible, which was to lose some of my tension."

Julie Hayes, in her late twenties, involved in a somewhat restive marriage to a *New York Times* correspondent who frequently travels without her, is about to be fired as a legman for a *Daily News* gossip columnist. Part of Julie's problem is that she has no consistent job for her own, so when she is dropped she sets up as a fortune teller in Times Square. In this first book, Julie has a running dialogue with her analyst. Davis has even more fun with Julie in *Scarlet Night*, a caper. The third Hayes book, *Lullaby of Murder*, was published in the spring of 1984.

Is there anything of Julie in Dorothy? Or vice versa? "In a lot of ways she's the things I'm not," Davis told me. "I have to watch my imagery because I come from a farm background, and she's strictly a city person. In Julie's next book, she is in search of her father, her roots. I went to Ireland to do the research for the book. In that way, I suppose that Julie's like me."

Does Davis propose to search for her own roots, back in Illinois?

"Someday, maybe. There is a certain amount of information available to me under the new laws governing adoptions, but I've never gone back to Springfield, Illinois, to get a court order that would open up the records to me."

Examining and introspective as they are, Davis's books haven't translated easily into the more active media. "Hitchcock did a couple of my short stories on his television series. *A Gentle Murderer* was bought for a feature film, but never made it. I've had a lot of stories optioned. Otto Preminger optioned *Dark Streets* for Frank Sinatra, but that project fell off the vine before it ripened."

Davis has been a member of the Mystery Writers of America since 1951 and has played an active role in it. She served as its president in 1956. She was executive vice-president in 1975–76 and again in 1977–78, during the Second International Congress of Mystery Writers in New York. She considers herself a "passive activist" as far as the woman's movement goes.

"I've been sympathetic," she told me during a December 1983 interview. "I suppose when they started, I felt, 'Gee, I'm doing all right in a man's world; what do I need this for?' But then I came along. I knew Betty Friedan, who was living near me in Rockland County when she wrote *The Feminine Mystique*. I think that the movement has gone hither and yon and sometimes has been quite ridiculous. I, for one, don't want to be a 'chairperson.' I don't even want to be a chairwoman. On the other hand, they have made some valid points."

How have these "points" influenced Davis's own writing? She says she is consciously raising the role of women in her own fiction.

Gestation period for a Davis book can be from three months to two years. "It depends on how long it takes me to get it going. It never takes two years to write. To rewrite, maybe. I throw a lot away. In fact, I once threw a completed manuscript away!

"I do a lot of research on each book. I walk a lot. I read a lot. I find myself copping out, running off to the library. Then there finally comes the point at which I must say, 'You've read enough; you ought to be able to do it!' Perhaps that's endemic to the business of writing mysteries."

Living close to New York, the Davises enjoy visiting in each others' worlds—mystery writing and show business. Harry Davis is no great mystery reader, but he enjoys mystery writers, while Dorothy has been known to use a show-business background in her writing, notably with Julie Hayes.

I asked Davis if there is anything special that she would like to write.

"I don't think there is. I've been writing for thirty-five years. I'd like to keep writing, but I'd be willing to say, 'All right. If I never write another book, I've done it!'

"However, I used an old country lawyer as the protagonist in two of my short stories. I kind of like him, and I may use him in more stories."

A Gentle Murderer

"Bless me, Father, for I have sinned." Father Duffy, assistant pastor of St. Timothy's Church, one of Manhattan's largest parishes, hears the phrase over and over as he listens to confessions on a Saturday evening in August. It is after 9 P.M., but the summer heat rolls into the small confession booth in waves.

"Father, I think I've killed someone!"

There is a young man in the confession booth, a man with a small, worn face.

"Father, I've always wanted to do some good in my life—I wanted to be a priest. I was always welcome up there—she was kind to me. I took a hammer with me. . . . My mother gave me a hammer for my tenth birthday. It was the only present she ever gave me. Father McGohey gave me a prayerbook for my first communion, then he took it away from me for fighting."

The desperate rambling narrative breaks.

"Father, absolve me please, and let me go."

It is then that Father Duffy notices the hammer. "There is a penance you will have to do according to the laws of society beyond any I can give you. . . ."

The young man's eyes stream with tears.

"You will go to the police now?"

Father Duffy receives no answer; the young man nods. Then he is gone.

Father Duffy returns to his rooms. Will the young man go to the police? The priest turns on the radio: on this particular stifling August night, among the global tragedies of the 1940s, fears and fiascoes, Metropolitan robberies and rescues, pathos and nonsense, murder in New York is not among them.

In the boarding house in New York's Greenwich Village there is a party going on when Tim Brandon returns to his room. Mrs. Galli and her friends have raucous entertainments; occasionally the Widow Galli tries to tempt Tim to join them, but he always resists her attempts. This evening there is a knock on his door.

It is Katie, Mrs. Galli's young daughter, who tries to get Tim to come down to the party. He refuses. They talk; there is real affection between them – the young man and the girl on the edge of womanhood.

During their conversation the reader discovers that Tim is a poet who works as a carpenter in a local shop. Katie is worried about him now; he has great hollows beneath his eyes and his body is awash with sweat. His good shirt is missing, too. She knows he has only two, and she washes and irons them both. She notices that his hammer is out of his tool kit; she replaces it for him. The hammer has a strange smell to it.

Father Duffy says his 6 A.M. mass the next morning, then returns to his room. He goes over the conversation with the young man not twelve hours before. His mother has given him a hammer. Father McGohey has given him a prayer book.

Perhaps it is all a hoax: there has been no murder at all. There are ways of identifying a man, though. The police look for fingerprints. Father Duffy goes to the rectory basement, locates a screwdriver and goes up to the confessional booth, where he removes the small board on which the "murderer's" fingerprints have been pressed the previous evening, and carries the board to his room.

In a fashionable Upper East Side apartment hotel later that morning, Norah Flaherty, housekeeper, is going about her work. She hopes to finish quickly and get home to her kids. She has knocked at 4-B several times, has received no answer, and has gone and done other apartments. Now it is half-past twelve. She lets herself into 4-B. If Miss Gebhardt isn't up yet, too bad; the work has to be done. The bedroom door is partially closed. Norah cleans up the kitchen and the bath. The slippered feet of Miss Gebhardt are visible to Mrs. Flaherty beyond the bedroom door. She finally pushes open the bedroom door. A sickening odor emanates from the room. Mrs. Flaherty tiptoes toward the bed, and suddenly realizes she is seeing all that there is left of Miss Gebhardt's face. She runs screaming into the hall.

The early afternoon edition of the tabloids carries the story. Dolly Gebhardt, an attractive redhead and former showgirl, has been bludgeoned to death with a hammer, and has been discovered by the hotel housekeeper.

Father Duffy reads the piece, his heart pounding. He knows

Norah Flaherty, one of his parishioners. And he knows that the man who entered his confessional booth was Miss Gebhardt's murderer. He looks up Norah's address in the parish registry and pays a visit.

Norah has become something of a local celebrity. She is queening it around her kitchen table, giving the neighbors tea and a goodly concoction of narrative gore and horror.

She tells her story again for Father Duffy.

Has she ever seen any men in Miss Gebhardt's apartment? She tells him of one young man that she has seen there; from Norah's description, Father Duffy feels that she is describing his penitent.

"You've never seen the man around St. Timothy's, have you?" He describes the young man. Norah is shocked at the idea. She is sure that the man Father Duffy describes isn't the murderer. She knows him; he's too gentle.

Lieutenant Holden and Detective Sergeant Goldsmith of the New York Police Department are in their office, looking at the autopsy report. "The blunt instrument. Hammer." They are discussing Dolly Gebhardt's murder. She, it turns out, is a high-priced call girl.

They trace the steps of her last day. She went out buying a new fur (the shopping bag is found in her apartment). She was dressed to the nines. Went out about seven, flagged a cab, but according to hotel personnel, was back in half an hour, saying she was ill. The cabbie helped her upstairs, then came down.

The officers have found the shirt the murderer wore: cheap, old. But the collar was starched. Someone was taking very good care of the man with the hammer.

In the oppressive heat of his Greenwich Village room, Tim lies on his bed. Mrs. Galli comes into his room, bringing him food. She pushes his papers back and tries to entice him. This has happened before, repeatedly; once Tim surrendered to her—but was disgusted with himself and filled with loathing at himself for letting it happen. Mrs. Galli is jealous of Katie. She rails at Tim for looking at the young girl the way that he does—but that is all that Tim has done: looked.

Trapped and desperate, Tim yearns for the woman to leave.

Father Duffy reads two stories in the next issue of the daily tabloid: Mr. Gebhardt has refused the body of his daughter for burial in Minnesota; and the cabby who drove the redhead is wanted for information about her last evening.

Father McGohey, the priest remembers. Perhaps he was a chaplain in World War I.

The cab driver is located and found to be innocent—and also none too helpful.

Holden and Goldsmith are awaiting the arrival in their office of Edgar G. Winters, the unhappy owner of several of the sets of fingerprints in Dolly Gebhardt's apartment. He is, apparently, Dolly's "sponsor," buyer of the newly purchased fur piece.

Day by day the story moves further back in the pages of the newspapers, the killer still undiscovered. Father Duffy locates a Reverend Walter McGohey's papers from the chaplain corps; the Reverend returned after the war to his parish in Marion City, Pennsylvania.

Father Duffy decides he can wait no longer. He has one week's vacation coming, a week set aside for fishing in Canada, but. . . .

One day later he is in Marion City, Pennsylvania, a coal-mining town. In a conversation with the parish housekeeper he discovers that Father McGohey has been dead some years. However, the housekeeper worked for him twenty years before, and she recognizes the "troubled young man" described by Father Duffy as Timothy Brandon.

At the local tavern Father Duffy gently primes the pumps to try to discover more about Father McGohey and the Brandon family. The miners tell him that Father McGohey fixed up a "gym" for the local lads. Duffy leads the talk to the Brandons. He finds that "Big Tim" Brandon was a worker in the mines. He was a famous drinker, and when drunk, often beat his wife, Mary, and their only son, "Little Tim." Father McGohey was very good to both Mary and Little Tim. The boy was bright and bookish, and when he was older, Mary Brandon was always writing away to seminaries to see if they would take him as a student. She finally got Father McGohey to help get Tim into a seminary. One oldtimer remembers the day Little Tim left. Big Tim watched the boy go off on the bus from this very tavern, and threw a bottle through the window at the bus as the boy stepped into it.

(The reader is left to surmise a great deal here. Was there more to the relationship between Mary Brandon and Father McGohey than that of priest and communicant? Was he kind to her and to the boy because Big Tim was a drunken wife-beater? Or was Big Tim a drunken wife-beater because of some relationship, real or imagined, between the two?)

Father Duffy leaves Marion City to visit the seminary that took in Tim Brandon.

Back in New York, Sergeant Goldsmith is following his own leads. He buys a drink for Liza Tracy, a singer friend of Dolly's. He discovers that Dolly has had lots of "johns" but, as with many prostitutes with hearts of gold, she has one special friend—a moneyless poet, a kind of pet charity. She entertained him in her home, gave him an occasional meal. The two made no more demands on each other.

Katie has gotten herself a job. It is so she can help Tim more. She has lied to her mother, saying she earns fifteen dollars a week; she is actually going to make about eight dollars more. She tells Tim she has gotten the job to give him extra money so he can spend more time on his writing and not have to worry about the rent money.

Tears well up in his eyes. "Dear, dear Katie." He hugs her to him.

Father Duffy locates one of Mary Brandon's sisters, who tells him that Big Tim is dead and that Mary Brandon is now a sister in a convent, where she is very, very happy.

Goldsmith is reading the poetry of Francis Thompson, a book he has found in Dolly's apartment. He now has a name for the man he thinks is Dolly's killer: Tim Brandon. He goes to Norah Flaherty and warns her that it is possible that Brandon might try to kill her.

Father Duffy visits the seminary attended by young Brandon. The seminarian tells Father Duffy that young Brandon was not cut out to be a priest. He also says that the boy's mother was an "unhealthy" woman. She worshipped the boy, but the letters she wrote her son were "disgusting." The boy was forever denying himself: no sugar on his oatmeal; a belt of thorns. He was allowed to go home for his father's funeral. The bursar gave him money. He came back in a week, but left the seminary soon after. He did not actually go to his father's funeral in Pennsylvania.

At the seminary, there is only one reminder of Tim's life. He left, among his belongings, a birthday card signed "Teddy," with a Cleveland address on it.

Father Duffy's next visit: Cleveland. There he finds a woman who befriended the young seminarian when he got off the train. It was during the thirties and there were lots of CCC boys going through to and from the work camps. The woman served in a canteen for one of them.

"He looked hungry; I fed him and then I brought him home with me. He stayed about a week. My daughter, Teddy, must have sent him that birthday card. She was only twelve. She adored him.

"It was obvious that he was very disturbed. He went back to the seminary, soon after came back, telling us he'd left it. My husband got him a part-time job at the library. He moved out, found a room over a blacksmith shop. There was a great tragedy about then; the juveniles' librarian was beaten to death one night going home from the library—with a hammer. Her husband was arrested, and killed himself in jail.

"The next thing I knew Tim was gone. The old blacksmith wept when he told me; he was so fond of Tim."

A sketch of Tim is made from Norah's description and distributed to various precincts. Goldsmith, visiting several editors of poetry magazines, locates one effete man whose magazine has folded, but who still has a check for five dollars for a poem he bought from Tim. Goldsmith takes the check with him.

Father Duffy returns to Manhattan. Goldsmith visits the theatrical boarding house in Greenwich Village where Dolly lived before she was set up in her posh apartment. He discovers that Tim also lived there. Slowly, Father Duffy from his parish and Goldsmith from his precinct find their way to the boarding house in the Village where Tim and Katie are about to leave town forever.

From page one the reader knows who the murderer is, but Davis's smaller mysteries-within-mysteries keep one haunted, and intrigued, until the final page, in which the murderer again whispers, "Bless me, Father, for I have sinned." Father Duffy, and Goldsmith, and the admirable Katie play their parts insistently in the life of the poet,

Tim, doomed early in his lifetime to become the gentle murderer.

Davis's fascination with the Roman Catholic ethic is evident in this story of innocence and guilt, of guilt and redemption, of flesh and fantasy. Her police work is impeccable, as is her sometimes ironic view of the workings of the Mother Church.

4

Lady Antonia Fraser

The Detective as Public Eye

There is a synergism about success; once you tap into it, everything you touch turns to gold. Such a fortune's darling is Lady Antonia Fraser, an Englishwoman who was born with a bountiful supply of good-fairy gifts and has managed to stockpile ever more such gifts into the sort of life that critics and columnists alike enjoy picking over in print.

Born fifty years ago into a titled, talented family, she has managed to be both talented and subsequently famous in her own right. After graduation from Oxford with a degree in history, she wrote a series of biographies that have been both critical and popular successes. She won the James Tait Black Prize for biography in 1969 (her mother had won the award in a previous year) for *Mary, Queen of Scots*.

Lady Antonia turned her pen to detective fiction in 1976. Her detective, Jemima Shore, a television personality, has been a great fictional success both in England and in the United States. Jemima made the transition to television, first in a mini-series and then as a series of thirteen weekly dramas. The mini-series, which was made from Lady Antonia's first book, *Quiet as a Nun*, was shown in America during the 1982–1983 season.

I was in London to interview three British writers for this volume, and was due to have lunch with Fraser the following day.

An old friend, Bettina McNulty, contributing editor to *House & Garden*, had come to the St. James Club for tea.

"Tell me what you know about Lady Antonia," I said to Bettina. "I came over to England in such a hurry I didn't do basic homework about her."

Bettina thought a minute. "Larger than life. Very tall and slim. Big blue eyes, big mobile lips. Transparent skin. Blonde. Fifty, and looks thirty." Bettina sipped her tea. "Lady Antonia has six children, and does all the necessary traffic duty that that entails: you know, shipping them off to school and back; helping with clothes, lessons; seeing about doctors, vacations, and on into advice about careers, love affairs. She has won awards for her biographies, now alternates the biographies with the Jemima Shore books. She adapted one of the books for the television series; divorced Hugh Fraser to marry Harold Pinter, the playwright. You're not going to lunch with a woman *that* busy and tell her *you* didn't have time to do your homework about her!"

I spent the evening with a copy of British *Who's Who* investigating the creator of Jemima Shore, Investigator.

She was born on August 17, 1932, in London to the Earl and Countess of Longford, converts to Roman Catholicism. Her father is a Member of Parliament, and is known affectionately in England as "Lord Porn," since his is the Parliamentary force behind the British antipornography laws. Her mother, Elizabeth Longford, is a noted writer of biographies. Lady Antonia spent two years at St. Mary's Convent School in Ascot before entering Lady Margaret Hall, Oxford, from which she received a degree in history.

In 1956 she married the Right Honorable Hugh Fraser, a Member of Parliament. They had three sons and three daughters. She is the author of biographies of England's King James, Charles II, Mary, Queen of Scots, and Oliver Cromwell, and has edited an anthology of *Love Letters*.

Her first novel, *Quiet as a Nun*, was published in 1977 and was written as "relaxation" from the nonfiction biographies. In 1976, in a spate of publicity, Lady Antonia divorced her husband to marry Harold Pinter, the playwright.

In my file was a small review of *Quiet as a Nun* from the *London Times*.

> In Jemima Shore we meet a character who is described in terms similar to those used about her creator by gossip columnists, and it will be tempting for future biographers to deduce this contemporary biographer's [Fraser's] tastes from her heroine's, who is defined, as James Bond was, by her taste in consumer goods. We know which dress designer she patronizes [Jean Muir], which tailor, hairdresser, parfumier and shirt-maker, and that she prefers to wear beige to go with her golden hair.[1]

Heads turned in the St. James Club dining room as the tall blonde in a teal blue Jean Muir suede dress was shown to my table. We introduced ourselves; my guest ordered a glass of white wine.

"Where did Jemima Shore come from?" I asked Lady Antonia.

"Barbara Walters was just becoming important in American television. When I was in New York I was struck by her fantastic fame. This phenomenon of fame has a lot to do with television. There was dead silence when the two of us entered a restaurant. People came up to her while we were eating and would say things to her—quite intimate things—and ask Walters's help in solving their problem. I thought, 'What a wonderful situation for a female detective.'

"When I began writing about Jemima we didn't even have a British woman reading the news on television. We now have a woman on our new morning news show, but she's not got the clout of a Barbara Walters.

"So Jemima was taken from the successful career women that exist in the States, and perhaps that's one of the reasons she's been so successful there. People recognize her without actually putting a name to her."

Was it an easy transition, going from biography to fiction?

"Yes. Quite easy. You know, there's a good deal of detective work tracking down facts for history."

"Is Jemima your alter ego?"

"She's not t'*tall* like me! Her private life is exactly the opposite of mine. She's single and she has no children. Do you have children?" she asked, as she toyed with her salad.

"Yes. Two."

"Then you know what I mean. I live in the world of children, and there's a profound chasm between those who live that way and those who don't. I married at twenty-four and had six children in ten years. I've lived in the world of children ever since. I hesitate to say which side of the chasm is better, because I wouldn't know. Jemima has made her own career, has a free-wheeling love life. Having said all that, I admit that there obviously are characteristics we share. For example, we are both cat lovers, and the cats in the Jemima Shore books are all taken from cats of my experience. Jemima and I love music—opera. Mozart, in particular. Her personal tastes are all taken from my own.

"Jemima is tall, has red hair rather than blonde. But I'm in the background, of course, because I write about things that I know about.

"The first Shore book, *Quiet as a Nun*, takes place in a girls' convent school, where Jemima went as a girl. I, too, went to such a school. And as Jemima says early on: 'That church training! Convent girls can run anything!'"

There are five Jemima Shore books to date.

The television adaptation of *Quiet as a Nun* was a great success in England, subsequently became a thirteen-part series. Jemima was played by actress Maria Aitken in the mini-series (*Quiet as a Nun*), by Patricia Hodge in the longer anthology series.

"I have very mixed feelings about the scripts," said Lady Antonia. "I had approval of the character, which I executed, so there's nothing alien in the character. The critics, beyond the adaptation that I did of *Splash of Red*, didn't like them. Some were kind and said they'd missed my touch; others said they didn't like my touch, but what came after was worse!" She shrugged her shoulders elegantly. "You know how critics are."

Do you have the same publisher for both your fiction and nonfiction?

"Yes. In fact, I was quite prepared not to. I told Lord Wiedenfeld, 'Look. Here it is. I am going to do more. But don't feel you've got to take the book. I'm quite prepared to go elsewhere with it.' He took it and the subsequent ones. So now I've something in common with Agatha Christie; we both publish mysteries under the name of a former husband."

Lady Antonia has three children still at home. There is a sixteen-year-old son at school, another son who's an apprentice journalist and a twenty-year-old daughter who's a theatrical agent. "The good thing is that all six children are close to each other. Six people, ten years—that's a very, very tight community."

The Pinters work in two separate spaces. "My husband has a mews house where he goes to write, whereas I have a sitting room where I work with a secretary. Only once did we share an office, my husband and I. It was on vacation. He was doing the screenplay of *Betrayal*. Harold never seemed to write *at all*. He would read the *Manchester Guardian*, walk about. Whereas I played Radio Three (the classical station) and wrote like a bat out of hell!"

(Note: the female lead in the movie *Betrayal* was played by Patricia Hodge, television's Jemima Shore.)

Who were the mystery writers most influential in Lady Antonia's writing?

"When I was growing up I read Dorothy L. Sayers's books. I read them over and over. I knew them by heart! Today, Emma Lathen is a favorite of mine. Could anybody *not* like Emma Lathen?"

Fraser is active in the British Crime Writers Association. Her favorite activity, though, is the English PEN Club.

"The club sponsored a colloquium between P. D. James and Ruth Rendell. I took a friend with me to hear it. It was extraordinary, really, the contrast between the two women. Phyllis James looking like the Queen, and my friend was sure that Rendell had been an actress, though I believe that this isn't so. Such presence, though! Phyllis has great presence, too, a different kind of presence. She's the American stereotype of the 'good British Woman.' Very chatty, nice and good-natured. Roars with laughter; rather bossy. I had to remind myself that this was P. D. James, the writer. I find both women inspirational."

As she got up to leave, heads in the St. James Club turned again. The well-bred soft buzz of the proper London dining room softened to pianissimo. Whether it was to watch the exit of a strikingly lovely blonde or the exit of Lady Antonia Fraser, one of the Beautiful People, I don't know. But it was a pretty fair approximation of the sort of attention paid to Barbara Walters as she exits from luncheon in New York's Le Cirque.

Quiet as a Nun

"Jemima Shore," says Antonia Fraser, writing about her detective heroine in *Murderess Ink*,[2] "is a combination of the repressed and the unrepressed. Jemima is a good seventeenth-century Puritan name, while Shore is taken from Jane Shore, the beautiful, dissolute mistress of Edward IV. Jemima—golden red hair, white skin, virginal air and many suitors—has many characteristics of that other intelligent, powerful woman, Elizabeth I of England."

Beautiful, clever, childless Jemima is a successful television reporter, with her own program, Jemima Shore Investigates, that looks into serious social problems. As a result of the billing, her viewing public has taken her more and more to be an amateur sleuth as well. Jemima has a well-ordered life, between home (an apartment in Holland Park Gardens) presided over by a worshipful daily, Mrs. Bancroft, and whichever cat happens to be in residence. Her office at Megalith Television is tended by an assistant, Cherry Bronson, whose curves are the toast of Megalith House. The current man in Jemima's life is Tom Amyas, a married liberal Member of Parliament.

Jemima reads in the newspaper that a nun has been found dead at Blessed Eleanor's Convent, Churne, Sussex. The sister, Rosabelle Mary Powerstock, forty-one, known in the convent as Sister Miriam, has been found dead of exposure locked in a deserted tower on the convent grounds. She apparently was unable to raise an alarm to call someone in to get her out.

The article takes Jemima back a whole generation to the time when she was herself a pupil at Blessed Eleanor's during World War II, a little Protestant day girl, bewildered and excited by the mysterious world of nuns and rich Catholic boarding students. Rosabelle Powerstock was a good friend.

A letter from Reverend Mother Ancilla arrives two weeks later. "Our girls nowadays regularly watch your program on television." The letter concludes with a plea for a visit from Jemima and her help in a "certain very delicate matter. Will you make time in your busy life for us?"

On a brisk fall day, Jemima drives to Churne and is shown into the Nun's Parlor to await Mother Ancilla. The walls are covered by holy pictures in reproduction, and on the table lies the familiar pile of wedding photographs of old girls, dating from Jemima's day, and enjoyed vicariously by the current "brides of Christ."

Mother Ancilla greets Jemima and begins her story. Rosabelle—now known as Sister Miriam—has had a decline in health, culminating in an emotional outburst in a classroom. She was whisked away to a sister house of the convent in Dorset, where, after six months, her composure returned and she came back to the Convent of the Blessed Eleanor to undertake light duties.

But Sister Miriam began to talk of visions; she ate less. One day she disappeared from the community. A typed note was found. It read: "I can no longer hide from the community that I have lost my vocation. I have gone to London. Please don't try to find me."

But Sister Miriam never went to London. She went across the grounds to Blessed Eleanor's Tower and locked herself in, where she died. One sister, however—Sister Edward—apparently knew of Sister Miriam's whereabouts, but never told. She was young and believed the older nun when she spoke of her visions and of her desire to purge herself of evil in the tower. Then, when Sister Edward realized the key to the tower had broken in two and Sister Miriam had lain there unable to get out, she nearly had a breakdown herself.

"Jemima," said the Reverend Mother. "You've got to help us find out why she died."

She hands Jemima a note in Sister Miriam's handwriting that says, "Jemima will understand what is going on here. Jemima knows why I have to do this."

The note has been found in Sister Miriam's missal.

"You didn't know that Rosabelle Powerstock was an heiress?" asks Mother Ancilla. "Her father was once Lord Mayor of London. It was he who bought all the buildings here and donated them to us originally. All the Powerstock money from generations back finally devolved upon Sister Miriam."

Jemima puts two and two together: Powers Square, Powers House in London; and the Powers Project fanatics and their leader, Alexander Skarbek. Everyone wants something different from the Powers Estate. In the struggle to provide low-cost housing in London, everyone has gotten into the act: Jemima produced a program on all of the factions involved and called the show "Powers Mad." The nuns and the girls alike watched the show, absorbed in it.

At the time of her death, Sister Miriam still owned the land the convent was located on. Although all nuns give up their worldly goods (and Sister Miriam gave most of hers to the convent) the Powerstock lawyers saw to it that she retained the deed to the convent land. And when she saw Alexander Skarbek on Jemima's show she decided then and there to give him the land for his low-cost housing project.

In the normal course of events, when Sister Miriam died the land would have gone to the convent, since she was the last of her line. She, who in her life never showed the slightest interest in her wealth, and who brought a substantial dowry to the convent, was now determined to bequeath to this Skarbek group the very land on which the convent rested. Her illness played strange tricks on her; she wrote a letter to Skarbek, offering him the land. However, nothing happened, because it was at this point that Sister Miriam died.

There were rumors of a final will that she had made, but no will has been found.

"Jemima, will you help us?" pleads Mother Ancilla.

Jemima reserves her answer. She is led out to lunch by Sister Edward, the nun who unfortunately did not reveal Sister Miriam's crazy plan of self-purgation.

"She killed her!" whispers Sister Edward to Jemima. "She wanted her dead, so she killed her!"

"Who?" asks a shocked Jemima.

"Why, Mother Ancilla, of course." She skims down the corridor like a small black bird. But from the back, she might be any nun, so alike do they all look to Jemima.

Gradually Jemima meets the other sisters. There is Sister Agnes, young, sweet-faced, and a cousin of Sister Miriam's on the maternal side—therefore not in line for any of the Powerstock money. Sister Agnes warns Jemima to return home, that she will find nothing to her advantage at the convent.

The following morning Sister Edward, who is an asthmatic, is discovered dead in her bed, medicines all within reach. Apparently she has been unable—for some reason—to take them.

Apparently she is dead of natural causes. Her older sister, a special friend of Sister Miriam's, left the order a year earlier. Later, two convent students, Margaret Plantagenet and Dody Sheehy, speak at dinner. "I wonder if anyone saw the Black Nun last night?"

The Black Nun is a school tradition. She is supposed to walk shortly before or after the death of a member of the convent community.

Jemima laughs at them, but some of the girls insist they saw the Black Nun three nights after Sister Miriam ran away . . . a strange nun, a nun without a face.

Next morning Jemima finds a typed note on her newspaper. "If you don't believe in the Black Nun," it reads, "why don't you come to the tower one night to see for yourself? Tomorrow night, for example."

Jemima resolves to go to the tower. She cadges a ride into Churne with Sister Lucy, the Infirmarian, who needs to have a prescription made up for one of the girls. They make the trip in a battered mini-traveler, Sister Lucy's dowry when she entered the order. Jemima buys a flashlight.

In the afternoon she invites Sister Elizabeth, the English teacher, to investigate the tower with her. The two climb the precarious stairs to the tower room and are shocked when they arrive. Draped in a rocking chair, looking like a live nun, is an empty nun's habit. Is that what the note means? Or will the habit be filled with a corpse in the evening?

Forewarned and forearmed—with flashlight and candles—Jemima sets out alone, in the dead of night, for the tower. She crosses the grounds, opens the door, ascends the stairs, and is attacked on all sides by a horrifying flight of bats. Fighting down her terror, she goes outside again to compose herself. She has lost her flashlight in the fracas, but lights one of her candles. She reenters the tower and hears a gentle rocking upstairs. Fearfully she pushes up the trapdoor. There, gently rocking to and fro in the chair is a nun. Beneath the white band of the wimple there is—nothing. A blackness. A void. Jemima screams, faints, and falls to the floor. . . .

Sister Agnes's face hovers solicitously over her own as she comes to.

"What are you doing here in the tower, Sister Agnes?" asks Jemima.

"My dear child, this isn't the tower; it's the chapel." How has she gotten from the tower to the chapel? Jemima spends the night in the infirmary.

At Sister Edward's funeral Jemima meets Beatrice O'Dowd, who left the community the previous year—a florid, overblown woman, hairstyle over-bouffant, lipstick too bright. How difficult it must be, thinks Jemima, for a woman to have to learn about hairstyles and makeup well into her middle years.

It turns out that Beatrice O'Dowd was a "particular friend" of Sister Miriam's. The phrase describes a close relationship between nuns. "Did you know, Jemima," Beatrice asks her, "that this abbey was founded on a 'particular friendship'? That of the Blessed Eleanor and Dame Ghislaine le Tourel. And yet Sister Miriam and I were denied even the simplest of human relationships and taught to consider it wrong."

The Christmas Bazaar takes place in early November. Lady Polly Justin, mother of Tessa and Mandy, is scheduled to open and close the fête, and to be handed a bouquet by her daughter, Tessa.

Mother Ancilla has a heart attack and is absent from the festivities. Her place is taken by Sister Boniface, the oldest sister of the community.

The Justins are upset. Tessa is nowhere to be found. As the fête rolls to a close her parents become apprehensive. Then her younger sister, Mandy, produces a typewritten note from Tessa found in her room. "I've gone to stay at my aunt's," it says. "I have plenty of money; don't worry about me."

But Sister Boniface points out that Tessa doesn't know how to type.

"Sister, is there a tunnel that connects the chapel with the tower?" Jemima asks Sister Boniface.

The old sister admits there is such a passage.

"Show me where it is."

In the sacristy of the altar, Sister Boniface opens a heavy oak door and shuts it firmly behind her and Jemima. They go down interminable steps to a crypt, where former reverend mothers are buried. And behind the coffins in the crypt, there is an iron grille, which the sister motions Jemima to enter.

This is a classic detective puzzle with all the important participants in a "closed circle" – in this case the school of Blessed Eleanor's Convent.

Here, collected on the grounds of the school is a group of nuns living what Jemima considers to be an "unnatural" life. They range in age from thirty to seventy. Under their tutelage is an equally diverse group of young women – among them the grave, quiet Margaret Plantagenet and her chatterbox friend, Dody Sheehy, and Tessa and Mandy, the two Justin girls. To this quiet, esoteric landscape comes Jemima Shore, the epitome of Today's Woman. In some ways the book brings to memory a classic of Josephine Tey's – *Miss Pym Disposes*.

The witty, literate Tey, however, would never have had one of her heroines wandering around alone at night, waiting to be bashed in the head by an unknown hand.

"It was Ogden Nash, who invented the term 'had-I-but-known,'" wrote Jessica Mann, "for crime stories that concern foolhardy heroines who need only to be warned of danger to rush into it alone. As he put it in another verse: 'Had she told the dicks / how she got in this fix / I would be much apter / to read the last chapter.'

"Jemima Shore may be a middle-aged career woman, but she is certainly foolhardy."[3]

She trips along in the middle of the night to an assignation with an unknown letter-writer in a dark tower, in which a nun has already died under questionable circumstances. Our heroine gets zonked – what else? – on the head and awakens with a terrible headache. As indeed she should!

Nevertheless, the well-described panoply of convent life and Fraser's own thorough knowledge of the life of a media darling add a neat patina of verisimilitude to the book. The quirks of human behavior are of more interest than a puzzling plot and it is these quirks that Fraser assembles and examines with precision and wit. When she allows Jemima to drop her foolhardy "had-I-but-known" proclivities, we can look forward to a satisfyingly well-rounded sleuth. Even so, the collection of nuns and young girls in *Quiet as a Nun* is as satisfying as it is vivid.

5

Lucy Freeman

Genesis of the Whydunit

"A new genre, dubbed the 'whydunit,' has arisen which, in addition to the suspense built in discovering who committed the murder, also reveals what in the person's past inexorably compelled him or her to kill."[1]

Since the early fifties, Lucy Freeman has written fifty-six books. Her special interest is the "whydunit" mystery. In addition to three books featuring a fictional psychoanalyst as detective, she wrote one of the first in-depth books about the roots of a crime. Long before Truman Capote's *In Cold Blood*, Freeman's *Before I Kill More* was a best-seller.

Lucy Freeman was born in New York City. The family moved to Westchester County when she was six years old. After high school, she went to Bennington College in Vermont.

"I'd always loved writing," says Freeman. "I began keeping a diary when I was eight years old. At Bennington, I had a remarkable teacher who acted as a spur to get me into writing."

After graduation from Bennington, she worked for the *New York Times* for thirteen years as a reporter. During her last six years at the *Times*, she set up the newspaper's mental health beat. She was by then in analysis herself, the beginning of a lifelong interest in the subject of psychoanalysis.

"The reason I went to an analyst was a physical condition that wasn't responding to regular medical treatment. I had a sinus problem that resisted all known therapies. My doctor said, 'Why don't you be a guinea pig and go into analysis?'

"I'd always been intrigued by what emotional disturbances meant, so I did. After three sessions on an analyst's couch my sinus condition disappeared. I found that once I was able to cry all my sinus passages loosened up!

"That, of course, was only the superficial aspect of analysis. There was a great deal more to the subject. I became fascinated with the study of my mind and the way I had concealed from myself all of my important feelings."

When she was twenty-eight, Freeman married a copy editor at the *Times*. The marriage lasted about a year and a half, then the two were divorced.

"Six years later, while I was still on the *Times*, I met a man who worked in Chicago. It was a traumatic period in my life: my father had just died; my mother was leaving the New York area. I chucked my job and went to live in Chicago with a new husband whom I scarcely knew. I stuck it out for a year and a half, then got my own apartment. I went back into analysis with a marvelous woman and during that period wrote my first book. It was called *Fight against Fear*, the story of my analysis, the solving for me of the mystery of mysteries—the depressions, the small murders that one commits upon oneself without realizing what is happening.

"The book was a best-seller. For its time, it made a lot of money, but every penny I earned went into psychoanalysis. Some of the money from the book paid for my divorce. I was under analysis for four years and during that time I wrote four books. Then my analyst died.

"I returned to New York, but I didn't go back to newspaper work. I liked the peace of writing books at home. So although free-lancing is a rocky way to live, I've managed it.

"I went into analysis again; it's been my personal and professional salvation. I have written extensively on Freud, on psychoanalysis, and I have used both in the books of fiction I've written."

Freeman's book *Before I Kill More* is an in-depth study—the first—of the roots of a real-life crime. In Chicago Freeman interviewed a young killer (dubbed the "Lipstick Killer" by the press) about his childhood, then interviewed his foster parents, his friends, and the teachers who had known him while he was growing up. Although the literary technique of returning to the roots of a crime has been done many times since (by Capote, by Flora Schreiber, by Tommy Thompson), Freeman's book was a first.

Her later excursions into detective fiction — three in number — feature a psychoanalyst, Dr. Ames, as detective. In the first, *The Dream*, the detective-psychoanalyst uses the symbols that recur in a dream to solve the murder.

"My plan was to show one psychoanalytic truth in each book. In the first I wanted to demonstrate the real meaning of a dream. I had the psychoanalyst solve the murder of one of his patients by getting to know people around the patient and then interpreting the last dream the patient revealed while on the couch — a dream that demonstrated tremendous fear of some unknown character.

"It was a fun book to write. It was published in paperback, and then adapted as a play. Unfortunately, as far as I am concerned, the playwright transformed the plot into a homosexual story, and not the story of a man murdered for the reasons he was murdered. The play folded in Philadelphia, and rightfully so — but I've got the program to prove that one of my books became a play!"

Freeman, a gregarious, popular member of the Mystery Writers of America (she was the 1984 president of the organization) lives in a sunny apartment facing New York's Central Park, which is her office as well as her home. She is currently working on a book with nonagenarian Dr. Karl Menninger of the famed Menninger Clinic in Minnesota.

"I owe him a lot," says Freeman. "His book, *The Human Mind*, made me and many others understand the murder in our own souls."

Freeman would like to get back to fiction writing, and hopes soon to write a psychological novel.

Some of her other books include *Freud and Women* (Frederick Ungar), written with Dr. Herbert S. Strean, psychoanalyst and distinguished professor at the graduate school of social work at Rutgers University. She edited and contributed to *The Murder Mystique* for Frederick Ungar. With Tennessee Williams's mother she wrote a book entitled *Remember Me to Tom* (G. P. Putnam & Sons). In 1974, Freeman edited *Killers of the Mind*, the annual anthology of the Mystery Writers of America.

The Psychiatrist Says Murder

As the new patient enters his office, Dr. Ames, New York psychiatrist-sleuth, has the feeling he has seen her before. She is a glistening blonde with thoughtful gray eyes.

"Do I lie on that?" she asks, indicating his couch.

"Why don't you sit here?" He points to a tweed armchair.

She is here, she tells him, because her husband hates her and wants to kill her.

Ames knows that the husband, Al Garth, is a successful Wall Street broker, somewhat older than his wife's twenty-nine years. She has been leading lady and dancer in a musical show.

Ames's patient tells her story. She and her husband had a whirlwind courtship, a honeymoon cruise. During the cruise Garth got drunk and beat up his bride in their cabin. Since that time, he has been drunk often and has used Helene as a punching bag.

"Why don't you leave him?" Ames asks.

"I hate to give the marriage so little time—less than a year. And then—sometimes, when he isn't drinking, he's tender and the sex is very good."

On the verge of tears, Helene tells Ames a bit about her family. Her father is dead. A wealthy manufacturer, he left Helene, her mother, and her brother, Evan, each well off. Her mother lives in New York, as does her brother, an artist, once married, once divorced.

At her next session Helene continues her story. Her husband has accused her of "cheating" him. Since she has not cheated in the ordinary sense, she doesn't know what he means.

Dr. Ames can guess. If a man feels a woman has "cheated" him, he unconsciously means she has failed to arouse him sexually. An emotionally immature man, Al Garth, who has to rely on his fists, not his virility, has imagined that a lovely young woman like Helene would make him potent. When she did not—no woman could—he felt enraged and so accused her of "cheating."

Garth was married and divorced before. His ex-wife, Marietta, lives in the city. Their daughter Amy is a freshman at Vassar.

The night before the second session Amy comes to dinner at the apartment. Al is drunk and embarrasses Helene in front of Amy.

Dr. Ames questions Helene about her parents. She adored her

father; Evan loved their mother. Once, when she was small, her beloved father beat her, and it was her brother who came late at night into her bedroom to comfort her. And once—when Evan was about ten—he and his best friend were caught comparing penises by the other boy's mother. All hell broke loose; Evan's father beat him unmercifully.

The following Monday Helene is late for her third session. When she finally comes in, she is walking like a zombie. Al Garth has tried to kill her. Drunk the previous evening, he raised his fist to hit her. When she ran out on to their terrace, eight floors above the street, he followed and almost succeeded in throwing her over the railing. Then he passed out.

Helene packed a small suitcase and fled to take a room in a hotel. The next morning when she returned to the apartment to pack her clothes she found Garth waiting for her. He was apologetic, penitent. He loved her, wouldn't let her run out on him. They made love—passionately.

Helene told him she was going to leave him anyway. He warned her that if she did he would come after her and kill her.

Hearing this, Dr. Ames advises specific action. The sooner Helene leaves Garth, the safer she will be. She must leave him today. She assures him she'll do it, and he hears a new strength in her voice.

But next day, Dr. Ames receives a phone call from Lt. Lonegan of the 19th Precinct. Ames once helped Lonegan solve a murder case, the victim one of the doctor's patients. Lonegan now asks his help once more: another of his patients is involved in murder.

Ames's first thought is that Garth has killed his wife; he expresses this idea to Lonegan.

"You on junk, Doc?" asks the officer. "It's the other way around. Albert Garth has been stabbed to death!"

Ames finally agrees to devote a full day talking to each of the people involved in Helene Garth's life, and will let the lieutenant know the results of the interviews.

Lonegan gives Ames a list of people: the first wife, Marietta; the daughter, Amy; Helene Garth's mother; her brother Evan; and Helene Garth's boyfriend.

"Who is her boy friend? asks an astonished Ames.

"Noel Marvin. An actor who was in her last show."

None of the suspects, Lonegan says, has a verifiable alibi for the previous evening. Of all the suspects, Helene Garth is the lieutenant's favorite.

The following afternoon Helene walks into Ames's office. She tells the doctor that the police have questioned her for hours. It was she who found her husband's body. She had gone to bed early; her husband was out attending a meeting. When she awoke in the morning she saw that his bed wasn't slept in. In the living room she found his body on the floor, blood all over it and on the white carpet.

"Could your husband have brought someone home with him?" Ames asks.

Easily, Helene says. The apartment has self-service elevators. And the night doorman takes off about once every hour to get himself a beer down the street. Someone could have come in with Garth and left without anyone's knowledge.

Why didn't Helene leave Garth, as she promised Ames she was going to?

Helene is disconcerted. When she went home from her session with Ames, Garth cried and begged her to give him one more chance. She agreed.

Ames asks Helene about Noel Marvin.

Helene says she was too embarrassed to tell him about the actor with whom she was in love. "Why *couldn't* I break away from Garth?" she asks Ames.

"Because you felt bound to him as in childhood you felt bound to a man like him. Your father. He too was alternately cruel and loving."

Helene tells Ames about a dream the previous night. She and her brother were running along a beach. She stopped to pick up a beautiful shiny shell. She put it in a little pocket inside the bra of her bikini. Evan shouted "Look!" He pointed to a black slimy object rolling in on the tide. It was obscene: a dead octopus with its tentacles cut off. Helene didn't want to look at it. The two of them buried the dead fish. End of dream.

Did she know what it meant? Ames asks her.

The slimy tentacles, the octopus, might represent the husband who had tried to choke her, she reasons. "Dreams use primitive symbols. The language of the dream is the language of the child, the savage."

She continues: as a child she and Evan had scoured the beach for shells. One day she found a sharp shell and insisted on carrying it home. She cut her hand on it; stitches had to be taken to stop the bleeding.

The next day Dr. Ames begins interviewing the people in Helene's life.

He discovers that Al Garth had strong ties with the homosexual community—ties that he tried to repress. After talking to the people involved in Garth's life, Ames decides that the murderer has to be one of two—Noel Marvin or Helene's brother Evan.

One evening Ames is shadowed, followed home through Central Park where he is viciously attacked. A woman and a policeman come to his rescue. Ames hurries to Helene's apartment. He knows now who the murderer is, and he knows that Helene is in danger.

Freeman uses one psychological truth in each of her Ames stories, making it the basis of the murder and of its solution. Here, the questions about homosexuality—overt and covert—are called into play. Freud's theory is that paranoia is a defense against homosexual desire; Ames feels that this theory explains Garth's behavior toward his two wives.

Freeman has spent most of her professional life involved with Freud's theories. To her, his word is gospel. And what she has to say about his theories both in her fiction and her nonfiction books is always provocative. However, in the past fifteen or twenty years many psychopharmaceutical drugs have been developed that have successfully treated mental illness. The biopsychiatrists who prescribe these medications feel that much mental illness has physical, rather than psychic, sources.

The jury is still out on whether paranoia is rooted in events that happened to the patient in infancy or childhood, or instead results from some chemical imbalance in the makeup of neurons, brain cells, and so on, or whether madness is perhaps some chance blending of both sets of circumstances.

The Ames stories, in which Freeman demonstrates one Freudian theory in each book, are not the multilayered studies in mania presented by Margaret Millar and Ruth Rendell, nor are they as richly faceted as Freeman's nonfiction books on aspects of psychology.

However, they are well-thought-out Freudian problems and are interesting as such, and good reads.

6

Dorothy B. Hughes
Escape and Pursuit

In the year 1954, the Mystery Writers of America presented a new and prestigious award, the Grand Master. The need for it was apparent. Some of the great names in the world of mystery writers had never received an Edgar for best mystery, or for best first mystery, yet were as important to the genre as those who had. The new honor would be given for an entire body of an author's work. The first Grand Master award went to Agatha Christie. In 1978, three Grand Master awards were given: to Dame Daphne du Maurier, to Dame Ngaio Marsh, and to Dorothy B. Hughes.

Mrs. Hughes, now in her eighties, with great-grandchildren, has been writing since 1931, when a book of her poems won an award in the Yale Series of Younger Poets competition. Three of her suspense books have been made into motion pictures still occasionally seen on late-night television. In 1950, she received an Edgar for her reviews of mystery fiction, which have appeared in the *Albuquerque Tribune*, the *Los Angeles Times*, and the defunct *N. Y. Herald Tribune*. She has written a biography of Erle Stanley Gardner, and says that "right now I am again composing (in my head only) a novel. Whether it ever becomes a book is, as you well know, on the knees of the gods."[1]

Dorothy Belle Flanagan was born in Kansas City, Missouri. "I am strictly city. I'm a third generation Missourian. Kansas City had a population of 350,000 when I was born. We rode streetcars downtown to shop, and to go to the theater, concerts, opera in season. In fact, at age nine I rode the streetcar to school."

Hughes has a sister, Calla Hay, two years younger, a longtime newspaperwoman in Santa Fe, whose column "*Paso por Aqui*" has long been considered a high point in New Mexico journalism. Hughes's brother, Frank, eight years younger than Dorothy, was the one who introduced her to the mystery field. As a youngster he would come from the library with armloads of mysteries. Dorothy was reading "literature," and scornful of his taste, but sampled an E. Phillips Oppenheim, and became an addict.

Eric Ambler was the important influence in Hughes's career as a mystery reader and writer. "After reading and rereading *The Mask of Dimitrios* I knew a mystery could have style as well as tell a good story, and I began to give serious attention to composing a mystery."

Hughes attended the University of Missouri, and came east to Columbia University in New York City. ("I consider New York my 'other state,'" she once said.) Early in her writing career she worked on newspapers and wrote poetry.

After her marriage to Levi Allen Hughes, Jr., of Santa Fe, New Mexico, she settled in that city. She has three children, ten grandchildren and two great-granddaughters.

She also attended the University of New Mexico, and in 1939 she wrote a history of the first fifty years of the university. The following year, she launched her career as a mystery writer and as a reviewer.

The So Blue Marble was the first of Hughes's skillful stories of escape and pursuit, and won for her excellent reviews. "An unforgettable experience in contemporary sensation fiction," said critic Anthony Boucher. Hughes proceeded to write eleven books in seven years, all of them well received and three of them made into important motion pictures of the forties.

The Fallen Sparrow starred John Garfield and Maureen O'Hara, and concerns an American veteran of the Spanish Civil War, tortured in a prison camp, who comes to New York to avenge the death of the man who helped him escape, and thinks he recognizes the crippled, evil camp supervisor.

Ride the Pink Horse, which appeared just after World War II, is as important for its handling of social problems as for its mystery element. "Set against Santa Fe's annual fiesta and with Santa Fe's lush desert and mountain background, the story tells of the collision of the three societies that have fused in New Mexico (Anglo, Indian, Spanish) as it explores the mind of a murderer."[2] The motion picture made from the book starred Robert Montgomery and Wanda Hendrix.

"I used the cause of minorities in my poetry and short stories long before I wrote novels. Why? I think from two sources of equal importance. (1.) A deep, everlasting and abiding, born-in-the-bones hatred of injustice in any form. (2.) The injustice perpetrated on minorities was learned by osmosis from my parents and grandparents."[3]

In a Lonely Place was published in 1947. The movie starred Humphrey Bogart and Gloria Graham and tells the story of a screenwriter with a persecution complex who bursts into violence when he is wrongly accused of murdering a waitress.

"My books were always made into 'A' pictures," says Hughes. "I never worked on the screenplays for the books. I don't think it's a good idea to work on your own material. That way, the books were very well done. I did work in movie writing for a while, but I never was any good at it."

She received twelve thousand dollars when *Fallen Sparrow* sold to the movies.

"That was a lot of money in those days. Raymond Chandler sold his first book to the movies for two thousand dollars! I was never *that* hungry. I had a husband supporting me. I stayed home, raised children."

She had the same agent for forty years. "Blanche Gregory is the reason I did well with the sales of my movie books. I got fine contracts."

Since 1947, there have been three other Hughes mysteries. *The Candy Kid* in 1950, *The Davidian Report*, a spy story, in 1952, and *The Expendable Man*, in 1963, considered by many to be Hughes's finest book. She writes equally well from a masculine or feminine point of view, begins, as do so many of her sister writers, with, "What if . . . this should happen? Then this will happen. . . ." and she's off!

Mrs. Hughes has written a biography of Erle Stanley Gardner, and has consistently reviewed mystery fiction. In 1978 Hughes signed a contract for the reissue of some of her books. She was pleasantly surprised at the price the contract brought her.

"Five figures for reissues of books that originally paid me a thousand dollars apiece!"

Now a widow, Hughes travels often, usually taking one grandchild or another along with her. She spent most of 1983 living in London (with side trips to Paris) with her grandson, Kevin, has shared a trip to Disneyland with another grandchild, Hawaii with another.

"Oh, and I took one grandson with me to New York City, which I still love, shabby and dirty as it is. The night we arrived my grandson phoned his mother back in New Mexico and after a day seeing the sights of the city, all he could think of to say to her was 'Wow!'"

The Fallen Sparrow

The Fallen Sparrow, published in 1942, during World War II, is dedicated to

Eric Ambler,
2nd Lieutenant, Royal Artillery,
somewhere in England,
because he has no book this year

As Hughes has suggested, Ambler was her own inspiration in the field of mystery writing, and *The Fallen Sparrow* is in the Ambler tradition of hide and seek, pursuit and discovery.

Important in the machinations of all books of pursuit is the plot device that Alfred Hitchcock liked to call the "MacGuffin"—the secret plans, the stolen gems, or the documents that the characters in a story are after, unimportant in themselves, but vitally important to the people involved.

Hitchcock's explanation of a "MacGuffin" goes this way:

Two men are riding on a train in Scotland. The first asks, "What's that package in the baggage rack?"

The other answers, "Oh, that's a MacGuffin."

"What's a MacGuffin?"

"It's an apparatus for trapping lions in the Scottish Highlands."

"But there are no lions in the Scottish Highlands."

The first responds, "Well, then, that's no MacGuffin!"

In other words, the MacGuffin, although important to the machinations of a suspense story is, in Hitchcock's words, "beside the point," and "actually nothing at all."[4]

Hughes's MacGuffin in *The Fallen Sparrow* is a set of priceless Babylonian gem-encrusted drinking cups, the bounty for which will finance Hitler's war a bit longer, if his agents can find them.

The story begins in a Spanish prison cell. Kit McKittrick, politically idealistic New Yorker, who has joined the International Brigade, is in solitary confinement, tortured there for many months. Once a month, special attention is paid him by a visitor Kit thinks is from Germany, a man who approaches Kit's cell with the drag of a wasted foot, and who leaves him barely alive as he tries to make Kit give up the secret of the Babylonian cups known to be in his possession. The Spanish War has been over for two years now, but Kit has been kept in solitary to force him to give up the secret.

The book proper begins in New York City. Kit, with the help of his friend, New York City cop Louis Lepetino, has escaped from the prison camp, made his way to New York, where his mother, widow of a New York cop and now married to a Park Avenue magnate, sends him to recuperate on a Western dude ranch.

While Kit is there, his friend Louie dies in a fall from the window of the Hotel George in New York. Kit, afraid that Louis has been killed because of his friendship with Kit by agents still in search of the Babylonian cups, hurries back to New York to try to uncover the truth.

Kit goes to the Park Avenue apartment of his mother and stepfather, a man whose family is so important that there is a Wilhite wing in the Metropolitan Museum. The familiar German cook isn't there; instead there is a new German maid whom Kit doesn't know.

The city is filled with European refugees. Europe is now Fortress Europa, under Nazi domination, and social New York is doing its best for the cause, housing and entertaining the royals and socials from Paris, Oslo, Prague, Rome.

Kit's first stop is at the home of Barby Taviton, the fiancée he left years before when he joined the International Brigade to fight in Spain's Civil War. Kit has dreamed of Barby all the years he fought and was imprisoned. They had met when Kit's college friend, Ab Hamilton, had brought Barby to the school for a college weekend, and Ab (who had always been in love with Barby) had given her up to Kit.

This evening, the Tavitons are entertaining before a huge benefit dance for Refugee Relief. On hand are two men whom Kit doesn't know, but who remind him of the charnel house of Spain. They are the Skaases: an old one, bald, shawled knees; a young one, blond, arrogant. The older one, Dr. Christian Skaas, Norwegian chemist, escaped from a prison camp, had won the Nobel prize in 1928. The younger Skaas is his nephew, a Bavarian, who had to run from Germany when his uncle got away from Norway. They are friends of Prince Felix Andrassy, who arrived from Paris with his granddaughter. All four live in the same apartment house on Riverside Drive.

As the guests pour from the Taviton apartment to go on to the benefit dance, Kit's old friend Ab pulls him aside and says that Barby is too interested in Otto Skaas. Ab himself now works for the State Department.

Entertaining at the benefit is another lovely girl whom Kit knew when she was a child. Now a "society chanteuse" is Content Hamilton, Ab's younger cousin. Sharing the bandstand with her is a Spanish refugee violinist, José. Together, the two make music of heart-quivering beauty.

Dancing with Barby, Kit elicits from her the information that Content has just returned from a Hollywood screen test. He notices another beautiful woman, whom he thinks he saw on the train to New York, discovers from Barby that she is Toni Donne, Prince Andrassy's granddaughter. Barby goes on to say that all of her set and Kit's stepfather's, too, are involved with the refugees, trying to get them homes and jobs. Dr. Skaas is supposed to teach at the University of Chicago in the fall; Barby's father and Kit's stepfather are trying to get Otto placed in the Justice Department, where his command of languages might be helpful. The idea makes Kit's blood run cold.

Back at their table, Kit asks Barby to have lunch with him the following day. She says she is going skiing with Otto. Kit decides to get drunk. Ab can't go with him; he has to stay with the party and is returning to Washington the next morning. Kit and Content leave the party together.

First stop: Carlo's restaurant, an Italian pavilion known to both Content and Kit. Carlo is Louis Lepetino's uncle.

First thing Content reveals to Kit is that Christian and Otto Skaas are enemy agents. How does she know? She just *feels* it. "How do we know where the real Skaas is? Anyone with a slight resemblance can play a wheelchair part. I can smell phonies." Unlike Barby and the rest of the elite, whom Content feels are "ten carat suckers."

They talk about Ab's new position in the State Department. As a boy, Ab found his mother and the shotgun with which she'd killed herself, and consequently has been unable to touch a gun ever since. He was not able to bring himself to join the International Brigade with Kit, and is happy with his new position in the State Department.

Content tells Kit that Toni Donne, Felix Andrassy's granddaughter, had seen Louie fall from the window of the Hotel George. Andrassy apparently is at the center of the refugee ring in New York. Another member of the ring is Det, an old friend of Kit's father, who went to France, married, returned to New York, and now runs a chic hat shop.

It was at a party at Det's apartment in the Hotel George that Louie fell out the window to his death. Toni Donne saw him fall and testified to this fact. Content and José were hired entertainers at the party. At the time Louie plunged to his death, everyone had an alibi: Old Dr. Skaas was with Content. Otto was up in his room above (at the time the Skaases were living at the George) to change a stained shirt. Toni went to a window to get some air and saw Louie tumble from the window. What was a New York cop doing at such a party? He came with Toni Donne.

Returning to his stepfather's apartment, Kit goes to hang up his coat, discovers in one of its pockets a small leather wallet that Kit gave to Louie as a gift when both were youngsters. Who put it there? Content? Barby? Ab? Soft-footed Carlo? Someone wanted Kit to have it.

Next morning Kit pays a call at Det's hat shop. The beautiful Toni Donne comes through the curtains to wait on him. Kit tries bluffing: he has come for his mother's hat. "Mrs. Wilhite has no hat on order," says Toni.

Kit invites the girl out to lunch. She refuses. He tries another tack, asking to see every hat in the shop. Finally, Det, the proprietress, comes to the front of the shop. She knew Kit's father, she is happy to see Kit—but she turns to granite when he tells her he wants to take out her salesgirl.

Toni watches him leave the shop.

After too much to drink in the Oak Room of The Plaza, Kit goes to Content's brownstone and passes out.

His next stop: Poppa and Momma Lepetino's apartment on the Lower East Side. If Louis died because of a seashell Kit sent him from Spain, Kit has to know. He elicits from Louie's parents the information that Louis died "because of the cops."

Next stop on Kit's itinerary is Club 50, where Content and José perform. Owner of club: Jake Lepetino, Louie's older brother. Did Jake know how Louie died? Jake shakes his head; he'd know how to take care of whoever had done it. Kit looks around Jake's office, sees no seashell that he might have sent to Louis. They comment on Louie's love for beautiful women; Kit asks Jake if perhaps Louie had met Toni Donne and Barby Taviton at his club, and Jake says yes.

Kit begins his double brandies at the bar again, and is finally locked out of the club at 2:30 A.M. Instead of heading home, he goes to Content's apartment and is about to climb the front steps when he hears the sound of a dragging foot—the sound he'd so dreaded in the Spanish jail. He calls the sound that of Wobblefoot. Kit ducks down under the steps as the man goes into Content's apartment house. Kit climbs the fire escape to Content's apartment and raps to be let inside.

She lets him in, convinced he's drunk. He describes the man—but Content doesn't know who it is. He searches her apartment, but discovers that Wobblefoot isn't there. Meanwhile, all hell breaks loose in the hall. It is the police. Someone has reported a burglar climbing the fire escape. (Kit, of course!)

Content opens the door, covers for Kit, and all the doors of the apartment house open. Kit sees José's anxious face peering into Content's apartment.

The excitement dies down. Content gives Kit a drink, and he tells her that Louie helped him escape from the Spanish prison. "He'd have gone to hell for me."

She asks him why he wasn't released from prison after the war.

"I had something they wanted." The Babylonian Cups.

"And why didn't they take it from you?"

"You can't take knowledge from a man. He has to give it up."

And Kit hadn't. "They haven't given up," he tells Content. "They've sent Wobblefoot for me." Kit can hear him now. "Listen!"

"Someone's just going downstairs," she says, dismissing Kit's fears. She asks Kit if Ab is in danger.

"He's in dangerous work," Kit says. "He was interested in the Skaases and Prince Felix, and Toni Donne had been seen with Louie."

He returns to his stepfather's apartment. Elise lets him in and gives him two phone messages. Ab Hamilton has called twice from Washington. Kit sees her try to hide the baggage check that he knows must be for his trunk. When he gets his trunk, he assembles all the letters he has received from Ab, from Louie, and from his mother since he has been in the West. A pattern finally emerges: all the refugees arriving in New York about a year ago; Louie's news: "I've met a girl" (Which one? Barby? Content? Toni?); Louie's death. It rushes up into Kit's consciousness: he hadn't *escaped* from prison; he'd been *let go*! His jailers followed him every step of his tortured way to freedom. They'd killed Louie. Why?

Kit's next stop is the police station, to see his friend Tobin. Kit tells him that the police hadn't gone into each apartment in Content's building that night.

Puzzled, Kit visits Det. She tells him she is in his debt because he is his father's son. Toni is there; she invites Kit to dinner at her grandfather's apartment.

At dinner on Riverside Drive with the prince and his granddaughter is Det, the Skaases, José. The first thing Kit notices are—the cups! Beautiful golden chalises, goblets, each with a magnificent stone on its base. The prince has the diamond; Det, the sapphire; Toni, the emerald; Dr. Skaas, the luminous pearl.

If the stones are genuine, even these imitations are worth a king's ransom. The originals are without price. And they belonged to Kit! Sir Christopher would, one day, present them to the Metropolitan Museum, for everyone to enjoy. Sir Christopher, who had taken them from Gottlieb, had thought he was playing the chivalrous game when he'd left Gottlieb bound and trussed up, and had described him so his torturers would know the man to find. The leader didn't get the cups, would never get the cups.

"The Babylonian goblets," the prince tells Kit, have been in his family for five hundred years, "the most precious treasure of the Kings of Babel."

Kit plays the game, tells the prince that the cups ought to be in the Metropolitan Museum, that the prince would make a lot of money if he sold them.

"I will not sell them."

Why did they go to the trouble of recreating the cups insofar as they were able?

Kit and Toni go out dancing after dinner. She admits that she slipped Louie's wallet in his pocket. She warns Kit that he must be careful. He kisses her, wants to know when he can see her again.

Next morning, he reads in the papers that Ab has been shot in a Washington hotel, and that the police have called it suicide. Kit knows that Ab could never fire a gun!

He locks Content up in his Park Avenue digs. He is afraid for her life.

Visiting Tobin at police headquarters, he tries to convince Tobin, called to Washington as a courtesy on Ab's case, that Ab has not killed himself, that he was simply getting too close to the agents who were after the cups. The Skaases, Kit says, are the agents.

But the Refugee Committee brought the Skaases into the country! How, counters Kit, does the Refugee Committee identify a scientist arriving in the country?

Barby and Otto have returned from skiing, and Barby is very upset. She and Ab were engaged to marry. She is convinced that Ab has been murdered, and by secret agents.

Meanwhile, small, blonde Content continues to stay with Kit, share his bedroom (though not his twin bed). Next morning, Kit goes out to get his mail, sees the German maid slip one of the envelopes into her apron pocket. He finally gets the envelope from her, discovers it is from Ab, who says he has proof that some of the people they know are secret agents.

Kit goes to Jake, Louie's brother, who lends him his private plane. He takes off for Washington, where Ab's friends in the State Department are still convinced that their man committed suicide.

Returning to New York, Kit takes the one memento of his cups—a magnificent fire opal—and has it made into a pendant, which he gives to Toni, but she doesn't want to take it. He offers it in front of Otto and Barby. Toni finally takes the gift. At the table in the Club 50, Content and José join the group, Content stiff with disdain at Kit for giving the opal to Toni, José recognizing the stone as one from the real Babylonian goblets.

Kit is again invited to dinner at the prince's home by Toni, and he accepts the invitation. Det, his friend, warns him against going. He knows the pattern now. He will be invited to an empty room; all of the other players will be together, have alibis. Except that he will not be alone and unarmed.

Kit goes to the house on Riverside Drive. Present are the Skaases, Toni, Det, Content, and José. Now he knows the name of Wobblefoot—the one who is *not* present. The prince. "My poor friend," says old Dr. Skaas, "he was taken with a heart attack this afternoon, and is in the hospital."

After the table has wined with the spurious goblets, and dined, Content and José do their special number, "Tzigane." During the number, Kit feels Toni's hand on his shoulder. Silently they leave the room, and she leads him up the back stairs to another apartment. She whispers, "God go with you," and leaves him.

He enters the room, and there, sitting in front of the fireplace, Prince Felix awaits him.

Three sexy ladies, two apparent suicides, a fire opal, and a set of priceless goblets set in motion against a backdrop of international espionage, sound like the stuff of mystery at its very best. Mrs. Hughes has packed action into her every word, and the words read as well today as they did in 1942. The book was reissued as a paperback by Bantam in 1979 (as well as *Ride the Pink Horse* and *In a Lonely Place*). One can only say: get cracking, Mrs. Hughes. We've waited a long time for a new Hughes.

7

P. D. James

Ordinary Lives, Extraordinary Deaths

"Why are respectable Englishwomen so good at murder?" asks Jessica Mann in *Deadlier Than the Male*, her book about female crime writers. It is, Mann says, that they have an eye for minute detail so necessary in detection. "In the peaceful English countryside, where a calm God-ordained middle class remained untroubled by any stirrings of workers' discontent, death occurred but violence seldom encroached. A dark stain spreading on the Axminster or a neat bullet hole in the back of a dinner jacket was as far as the Englishwoman went to symbolize murder. A well-ordered society where right would prevail, the criminal never escapes—so different from the anarchy all around."[1] A tradition begun by Dorothy L. Sayers, Agatha Christie, Ngaio Marsh, and Margery Allingham.

One of the heiresses to the mantles of these women is P. D. James whose first novel, *Cover Her Face*, was published in 1962 when she was forty-two years old, and whose books—in one case, at least (*Unnatural Causes*)—poke gentle fun at what Dilys Wynn named the English Cozies, James being anything but cozy in her writing.

Phyllis Dorothy James was born in 1920 in Oxford. She had a sister eighteen months younger, a brother eighteen months younger again. Her father was a civil servant and the family must have been fond of moving because after Oxford they went to Ludlow, near the Welsh border, thence to Cambridge, her father transferring to another Inland Revenue office (like the IRS) with each move. James went to Cambridge High School. Cambridge is in fact still one of her favorite cities.

"I didn't have any further education. I wanted very much to go to university, but this was before World War II and there weren't any grants. My father couldn't afford to send me."[2]

When the war broke out, James went to work in the government food ration office. She married a medical student and moved to London. Eventually her husband went off to the war; when he returned he was mentally ill and unable to work. James had two small children to support. She then became a clerk in the National Health Service. When she realized that her husband probably wouldn't recover, she went to school at night and took courses to qualify in hospital administration.

James's husband soon died, and she brought up her daughters alone, supporting them first with her work in hospital administration and later with the Home Office, akin to the U.S. Department of Justice.

As a writer "I was a late starter," James says. "From an early age I knew I wanted to be a novelist. But I was nineteen when the war broke out, and I worked steadily from that date. When I actually got down to thinking about writing a book, there was no question of leaving my position to write it. Still, I felt that if I didn't get on with it soon there was the possibility that I would be a failed novelist.

"There never *is* a convenient time to begin, really, a time when you get all the materials together and then sit down and do it. You just have to begin."[3]

James got in the habit of getting up at 6 A.M. and wrote *Cover Her Face*. In it, she introduced her detective, Inspector Adam Dalgliesh, a published poet who has a tolerant distaste for the messier aspects of life and a striking absence of illusions about his own activity.

"I was, I think, influenced by Dorothy L. Sayers and by Margery Allingham. Sayers I had read as a girl, and Allingham has such a marvelous way of creating her setting and atmosphere."

"*Cover Her Face* wasn't an immediate success in terms that it suddenly burst upon an astounded public, but it didn't get a single bad review, so that from a prestige point of view it did well. I realized about one thousand dollars from the sale of the book, so there was never any question of retiring from my job.

"But it was a fascinating job! I worked in the Home Office, which added tremendously to the raw material I had to work with as a novelist. It brought me in touch with policemen, detectives, the entire machinery of the law. Before that job I was in hospital service, and *Shroud for a Nightingale* wouldn't have been as realistic as it was if I hadn't had that hospital background. There might be great advantages to being able to sit at home and write, but that wasn't true in my case."

It took five years for her to write a book, during which time she worked and lived with her in-laws while her daughters were at boarding school. *Shroud for a Nightingale* (1971), James's fourth book, was the one with which she might have retired from her Home Office position, but she stayed with the department until her official retirement in 1979.

The first three Dalgliesh mysteries were essentially conventional British mysteries. When James dipped into her professional background, her books moved onto another plane. *Shroud*, set in a Nurses Training School (and whose nurse trainees are reminiscent of an earlier group of wacky, endearing students at a physical training college in Josephine Tey's *Miss Pym Disposes*), opens with a bizarre murder, and it won for James the British Crime Writers' Silver Dagger and the Mystery Writers of America's Edgar Allan Poe scroll.

James next turned her talents to a young women detective, Cordelia Gray, who has her own detective agency, in *An Unsuitable Job for a Woman* (1973), later made into a film in England.

Innocent Blood (1980) was James's breakaway book, in that it didn't fit in the conventional mystery mold. The story is about an adopted girl who rediscovers her natural mother, and subsequently learns that her mother is a murderess. It was on the *New York Times* best seller list in both hardcover and paperback versions. According to Scribners, James's American publisher, close to a million dollars has been realized on *Innocent Blood* in this country alone, between book sales, book-club arrangements and motion-picture sales.

"It's kind of a difficult book from which to fashion a film," said James. She's correct. Twentieth-Century Fox bought the screen rights to it, signed Tom Stoppard to write the script and Mike Nichols to direct it. That all took place several years ago. *Innocent Blood* seems to be having one of those long gestation periods so common to some movies. Meanwhile, England's Anglia TV bought the rights to half a dozen of James's Dalgliesh stories.

Sayers's attention to detail was an astonishing thing. Equally careful research goes into James's books, from the technical aspects of an investigation (e.g., the scientific principle of electrophoresis described in *Death of an Expert Witness*) to the daily routine in a nursing home.

"There's a clue in something George Orwell said: 'Murder, being the unique crime, tends to the strong emotions.' I think women are very good at dealing with the strong emotions. We have an eye for detail, which is terribly important. We have an eye for minutiae and, after all, if you're clue-making that's also vital."

James now lives in a flat in London's Holland Park. She travels to the United States whenever one of her books is introduced here. She's an active member of the British Crime Writers Association. She has, to date, won two Silver Daggers (the other one being for *The Black Tower* [1975]) and is currently writing a play—not a mystery.

"Murder is essentially a domestic crime, in which we explore the effect of the extraordinary upon the ordinary. That's why many of us prefer to write about small towns or small communities. We don't deal with violence in the same way that the sharp-shooting private eye does. We are interested in the details of living. Whether or not we also have a lot of hidden aggression which we are sublimating, I wouldn't want to say."

Death of an Expert Witness

"One of the problems with having a Scotland Yard detective such as Adam Dalgliesh," says P. D. James in an interview with Patricia Craig, "is that, unless you're prepared to keep all his crimes in London, you have to invent a good excuse for getting him to work in another part of the country."[3]

And getting Dalgliesh—James's austere, fastidious poet-detective—around England is important to James, for whom places loom large.

"Very often," she continues in the Craig interview, "a place rather than a particular plot, and sometimes a place rather than a particular character, sparks off my imagination and gets a book started."

Death of an Expert Witness is a case in point. The story is set in a forensic science laboratory (the "closed community" so beloved of every good English fiction writer since Jane Austen and a convention in which James enjoys working) located in the bleak, sinister Fens of East Anglia.

Hoggatt's Laboratory, founded by Colonel Hoggatt in Chevisham Manor when he was Chief Constable in 1898, is the oldest forensic science laboratory in the country. It is still lodged in the colonel's Palladian manor house (though a new laboratory is being erected on the manor grounds). Its staff consists of Dr. Max Howarth, appointed director of the lab about a year before, who lives in aristocratic splendor with his beautiful sister, Domenica. Dr. Edwin Lorrimer is the senior biologist, withdrawn, unfriendly; he had hoped to have been appointed the head of Hoggatt's. His affair with Domenica is a secret unknown to his colleagues (though known to Howarth). Lorrimer's cousin, Angela, is Howarth's secretary; she lives with a writer friend—Stella—in a small cottage that the two wish to buy, but lack the cash. Though Lorrimer is Angela's cousin, he inherited all of their grandmother's money.

The senior pathologist is Dr. Kerrison. He works for the local law-enforcement agency as well as for the laboratory. A lonely man, he presides over the household that includes a neurotic sixteen-year-old daughter, a small son, William. His wife left him for another doctor a year ago, and he lives in fear that she will establish a home and sue for recovery of her children. He has, consequently, made an arrangement with a Miss Willard to live with them. She manages to cook them an indifferent evening meal but does not put herself out much at any other time for the Kerrisons.

In the reception room at Hoggatt's are Brenda Pridmore, the attractive young receptionist, and Inspector Blakelock, the avuncular police liaison officer.

Paul Middlemass, senior documents officer, receives a phone call from young Susan Bradley, who once worked for him. She is worried about her husband, Clifford, a junior biologist under Lorrimer, who is so terrified of working with Lorrimer that he can no longer adequately function in his job. Susan begs for his help in doing something for Clifford. Middlemass tells Susan not to worry.

In the laboratory he warns Lorrimer to go easy on Clifford Bradley, remembering another case in which Lorrimer rode an underling to suicide—a cousin of Middlemass's.

Words are exchanged between the two men, then Middlemass taunts Lorrimer:

"Look, man, if you can't make it in bed, if she isn't finding you quite up to the mark, don't take your frustration out on the rest of us. Remember Chesterfield's remark: The expense is exorbitant, the position ridiculous, and the pleasure transitory."

The result is violent reaction: the two exchange blows. In the fracas, Lorrimer's nose bleeds on Middlemass's white coat. The two back off, Middlemass goes into the men's room to put the coat in the laundry basket and to wash up.

At eight-forty the following morning, after a village concert, Brenda and Inspector Blakelock arrive together to open up the lab. The police deliver a parcel of items from the corpse of a young woman found in an abandoned chalk pit. The phone rings; it is old Mr. Lorrimer. He asks if his son is at the lab; he has not been home all night. Brenda goes up the stairs to check on Dr. Lorrimer. Almost alone of the staff, she actually likes him. The doctor has been more than kind to her, suggesting that she go on to school, that one day she might be a proper staff member at the lab.

Brenda enters the lab, discovers Lorrimer dead, his head smashed in by a mallet that he has apparently been examining. She flies downstairs to get Inspector Blakelock, and collapses in a chair.

The hall is filled with people who are arriving for the day. Mrs. Bidwell, the cleaner, is indignant at being late; earlier that morning her husband received a phone call from a woman instructing her to go to Mrs. Schofield's—Domenica's—to clean. The call was a hoax; she wasn't needed at Domenica's. Howarth, Angela Foley, and Cliff Bradley are all present when Blakelock comes down the stairs and announces that Lorrimer has been killed.

He phones the Home Office in London and requests that someone be dispatched to Hoggatt's to investigate the murder. The controller of the Forensic Science Service, who is in the hospital, is delighted to discover that his old friend, Adam Dalgliesh, is being sent from New Scotland Yard to Hoggatt's. Dalgliesh visits the controller in the hospital.

"Tell me about Lorrimer," says Dalgliesh. "What was he like?"

That is the question that lies at the heart of every murder investigation; and yet Dalgliesh knows its absurdity before he asks it. The victim is central to the mystery of his own death. He dies because of what he is. Before the case is finished Dalgliesh will receive a dozen pictures of Lorrimer's personality, transferred like prints from other individuals' minds. From these uncertain images he will create his own pictures, essentially just as incomplete, just as distorted by his own preconceptions, and his own personality.

"Aged about forty. Looks like John the Baptist without the beard and just as uncompromising. Single. Lived with an elderly father. Was an extremely competent forensic biologist, but I doubt he would have gone higher. Obsessional, edgy, uncomfortable to be with. Was runner-up to Howarth when we made the appointment, and he took the appointment pretty hard.

"Howarth, the new head, is pure physicist and an administrator. His marriage had broken up and he and his half-sister (both independently wealthy) were living in East Anglia."

For the good of the service it is important for the case to be solved fast. Dalgliesh and another officer, John Massingham, arrive by helicopter to find the doors of Hoggatt's locked and the staff occupied with writing accounts of their actions between 9 and 10 P.M.—the time Lorrimer was presumed to have been murdered.

And so they arrive by air "at an unsuitable Palladian mansion in an unexciting East Anglian village at the edge of the black fens, where winters freeze your marrow and a spring wind whips up the peat and fills your lungs with smog."

Dalgliesh consults first with Blakelock, in charge of security, discovers that only the front door is available for entrance and exit to the lab. On the previous evening all the doors were locked and an alarm system calculated to make a great deal of racket and linked to the local police station would have gone off if someone had failed to use the proper keys.

Dr. Kerrison has done the preliminary examination of the body and Dalgliesh interviews him first, discovers that Lorrimer was struck while his back was turned, the blow wielded by either a man or a woman.

Dalgliesh asks Howarth who has been alone with the body.

"Only Brenda, for a moment; then Inspector Blakelock for a few minutes. Then me. Then Dr. Kerrison examined the body. He suggested that I call in Dr. Greene, the local police surgeon to confirm his findings. Dr. Greene wasn't alone with the body."

Dalgliesh searches the corpse. Under his white coat Lorrimer wears slacks and a tweed jacket. In the inside pocket is a leather wallet containing some pound notes, a driver's license, a book of stamps, and two credit cards. The right pocket holds a pouch which contains his car keys and three other keys. In the bottom pocket is a handkerchief, a bunch of lab keys, and, not on the chain with the others, a single heavy key, fairly new.

Claire Easterbrook, Lorrimer's senior assistant, tells Dalgliesh about the work on which Lorrimer was engaged when he died. He was rechecking Clifford Bradley's work on the mallet used in a murder case, and confirmed Bradley's results. But a page seems to be missing from the workbook of the mediculous Lorrimer—the last page.

Dalgliesh next talks to Mrs. Bidwell, who takes him on a "cleaner's tour" of the manor. They go into the men's lavatory. Dalgliesh detects the faint acrid smell of stale vomit coming from one of the drains. Mrs. Bidwell looks in the laundry basket, expecting to see Middlemass's bloodied white coat; but it is missing.

Does Howarth recognize the keys in Lorrimer's pockets—the three together and the single key? The three are for the doors to the laboratory; Howarth thinks the single key is for the small chapel on the grounds, barely used. Howarth held a small concert there once, featuring the string quartet which he formed, and of which he was a member.

He had, in fact, been playing violin as a member of the village concert the previous evening during the hour that Lorrimer was killed.

Brenda Pridmore, fresh-faced, young and sweet, tells Dalgliesh about an incident two days before during which Lorrimer, in a pet, found Dr. Kerrison's two children downstairs waiting for their father in the entrance hall. He ordered them from the building.

Dalgliesh and Massingham go to the home of Lorrimer. The murdered man's father is there. Angela Foley came over to minister to her uncle's wants after Lorrimer's body was found; subsequently she sent for her friend Claire. Dalgliesh is disturbed to discover that Claire has been rummaging around upstairs in Dr. Lorrimer's room.

The old man tells Dalgliesh that the doctor recently received a phone call from a woman who read off a list of numbers to him. The old man remembers two of the numbers: 18, 40.

In the deceased's small room are about four hundred books, many of them metaphysical. Dalgliesh discovers a will in the desk, leaving the cottage to his father and the remainder of his estate to his cousin, Angela Foley. Also in the desk is a packet of erotic love letters. Dalgliesh is struck by the contrast of the tranquillity of the man's room and the turbulence of his mind. On a half sheet of paper is a single name, written again and again. Domenica. Domenica. Domenica Lorrimer—like a young girl practicing in secret the hoped-for married name. All the letters are undated; most seemed to be first drafts.

In a visit to Lorrimer's lawyer, Dalgliesh and Massingham learn that the doctor recently made a new will disinheriting Angela Foley, since he did not approve of her living with Stella Mawsom. He added a new legatee: Brenda Pridmore was to inherit a thousand pounds "to continue her education."

A red Jaguar and a Triumph stand outside Leamings, the impressive home where Max Howarth and Domenica Schofield live. Domenica is beautiful, restless, an artist. She and her half-brother look enough alike to be twins; she is so sensual that even Dalgliesh, usually immune to feminine beauty, feels a twinge.

She tells them that Lorrimer expected her to love him, but that "love is something I didn't have to give and he had no right to expect." Two months before she threw him over.

"When you'd exhausted possibilities, sexual and emotional?"

"Say intellectual, rather. I find that one exhausts the physical possibilities fairly soon. But if a man has wit, intelligence and his own enthusiasms then there's some kind of purpose in the relationship."

"Where did the two of you make love?" Clearly not her house, nor his.

She refuses to say.

Her alibi? She and her brother had an early supper, Howarth left home at seven-twenty for the concert. She continued working until her brother returned shortly after ten when they had a whiskey together and retired.

At Dr. Kerrison's, the two officers meet Eleanor, sixteen, and William, an enchanting young boy. And they meet Miss Willard, who smells of sherry and body odor and who takes very little care of the two children. "I'm not the housekeeper here, you see." Miss Willard drives Dr. Lorrimer back and forth to church occasionally, since both attend services at the same place of worship.

Brenda's bicycle has got two flat tires. Walking home, she goes through the unfinished building of the new lab. It is dark and she knows she is being followed. So she runs – through the new lab, and out, straight into the small chapel, now unlocked. It is dark in the chapel. As she moves through the building, she brushes against an object swinging from the rafters. Terrified, she pulls back and in the darkness sees the body of Stella Mawsom. Circling Stella's neck is a double cord of blue silk. Brenda pitches forward in a faint.

"Detectives are far more credible today," James told Mary Cantwell of the Associated Press in an interview. "The day is over of the amateur like Dorothy Sayers's Peter Wimsey playing Scarlatti without the score, able to dive from a fountain into shallow water, running rings around the slower wits of the police . . . readers expect a great deal more characterization and psychological truth in a mystery."[4]

Dalgliesh is right up there with Lord Peter, with Rory Alleyn, and with Albert Campion, the detectives of three writers James says were influential in her becoming a writer. Except that James has more insight into character; her characters are anything but stereotypes. Her books are literate, often witty, always intelligent, and each one is better than the previous.

8

Emma Lathen

The Business of Murder

Back in the early 1970s, after Emma Lathen had achieved some prominence on the publishing scene, C. P. Snow, the British novelist, wrote of her in London's *Financial Times*: "She is probably the best living writer of American detective stories. . . . The detail is investigated with the enthusiasm of Balzac. . . . She is witty in a wry, downbeat manner. Read the detective stories of Emma Lathen. They express much more of what a working America is like than any 'high art' I know of."[1]

It is now common knowledge that the "she" of whom Snow wrote is actually two women, and that their collaboration is so successful it has spawned a second mystery-story series under a second pseudonym.

"Emma Lathen" is actually Mary Jane Latsis, who holds a doctorate in economics, and Martha Hennisart, a lawyer. The two met at Harvard in the fifties where each was doing graduate work. They discovered that they both devoured mysteries, particularly those from the Golden Age.

"We said, 'Let's write a book, a whole series, with an attractive character; let's have him move in situations where we can use our own strengths.'"[2]

The immediate incentive was a three-thousand-dollar contest conducted by the Macmillan Publishing Company. The women didn't win the contest, but Macmillan accepted their manuscript, published it and their next six, whose industrial subject matter ranged from a grain sale to Russia (*Murder against the Grain*) to the medical industry (*A Stitch in Time*).

One of the reasons for the pseudonym (an acronym from the beginning letters of their last names, LATsis and HENnisart) was that both women were working at their professions during the writing of many of the books and they felt that if they were "known as the authors of books in which a good many pretentious bubbles get burst, their clients and employers might feel a bit uneasy."[3]

Hennisart, the lawyer, comes originally from New York. She majored in physics at college, worked in Washington, got her law degree at Harvard and practiced in both New York and Boston. Latsis comes from Oak Park, Illinois, majored in economics at college, worked in Washington and in Europe, got her Master's Degree in public administration at Harvard (now the Kennedy School of Government). Both women are now retired from their original professions and write full-time. They live in the Boston suburbs and spend summers in New Hampshire.

According to an interview with John C. Carr in *The Craft of Crime* (Houghton Mifflin, 1983), Latsis and Hennisart had read Allingham, Sayers, and Tey, as well as Chandler and Hammett. But the social comedies in which John Putnam Thatcher, senior vice president of the Sloan Guaranty Trust Company, solves his capitalist mysteries point to a lifetime background of reading that includes everything "from Jane Austen through Sherlock Holmes," in the words of Latsis.

In a literary world in which narrative has been an old-fashioned word for some years, it is a pleasure to read the almost Trollopian picture of a complex society presented by Lathen in books that cover industries or societies as intricate as those of the Olympic Games (*Going for the Gold*), a hockey franchise (*Murder without Icing*) — "we are hockey fans, and we go to the games" — and a seed company that has developed a tomato that is a horticultural, economic, and genetic miracle (their latest book — *Green Grow the Dollars*).

John Putnam Thatcher is the witty, urbane senior vice president of the Sloan Guaranty Trust. A *New Yorker* reviewer once called Thatcher a man of "great charm, bottomless suspicion and Euclidean squareness."[4] Thatcher is a Brooks Brothers–clad widower, complete with grandchildren. In the "third-most-important" bank in the world, Thatcher is the straight man in a zoo of pretentious buffoons. Brad Withers, the president of the Sloan (and a Yale man), is relegated to handling only the purely ceremonial functions of the bank—so inclined is he to goof up. Thatcher must cope with zany public-relations men, friends whose love affairs keep getting in the way of their business affairs, and, inevitably in each book, a murder or two. In these complications he is helped inestimably by Miss Rose Corsa, the world's most efficient secretary.

The first six Thatcher books were published by Macmillan; Simon & Schuster now does the Emma Lathen books.

Recently when Latsis and Hennisart decided to investigate the unique machinations that are a feature of the nation's Capital, they decided to use a second pseudonym, and create a second protagonist. Ben Safford, a congressman from a district in southern Ohio, became the hero of the second series, authored by "R. B. Dominic." This series focuses on low doings in high places. *There Is No Justice* (in which a nominee to the Supreme Court is done in), *Epitaph for a Lobbyist* (in which a lady lobbyist is slain at Dulles National Airport) are two of the titles in the series. Originally published by Doubleday, the R. B. Dominic books are now done by St. Martin's Press.

How do the women go about collaborating as Emma Lathen and R. B. Dominic?

They decide in advance on who is going to be murdered and who's going to do it and write a complete outline of the book. They then write alternating chapters—simultaneously—exchanging drafts and editing each other's work. A book typically takes them anywhere from seven months to over a year to complete.

All of the Lathen titles have been published in paperback. They are also reprinted in England and have been translated into German, Danish, Swedish, Norwegian, Dutch, and Portuguese. Lathen received the British Crime Writers' Silver Dagger in 1967 for *Murder against the Grain*.

At the 1983 Edgar Awards of the Mystery Writers of America, a new award was introduced in honor of Ellery Queen, to be given whenever the Awards Committee felt such distinction was warranted. Accordingly, the first Ellery Queen Award was presented in May 1983 to Latsis and Hennisart as Emma Lathen. The rationale for this award could not be more appropriate. "Ellery Queen" was the pseudonym of two cousins, Frederic Dannay and Manfred Lee, who wrote together for many years. The two also wrote under a second pseudonym, Barnaby Ross.

Both Ellery Queen and Emma Lathen stood docilely behind their "other names" for many years. It's fitting that all of them are now out in the open to receive the praise they so clearly merit.

Murder against the Grain

Gorky Park, a best-selling thriller of 1981, featured a cast of Russian detectives, villains, and victims crosshatched with American counterparts. Given the different ideological backgrounds of each group, it was amusing for the reader to observe how similar the reactions of both groups were to dark and devious actions.

Fourteen years earlier Emma Lathen performed the same literary legerdemain when she tackled US–USSR trade relations in *Murder against the Grain*, a book whose background is the first sale of United States wheat to Russia, and whose performance is laced with typical Lathen wit, tone, and charm.

"Basically, the situation is quite simple, Inspector," John Putnam Thatcher, senior vice president of the Sloan Guarantee Trust, in New York's Exchange Place, is telling Detective Inspector Lyons of the New York Police Department. "It's as if someone had passed a forged check. Unfortunately, the details are a little more complicated."

Reducing the intricacies of foreign trade to bare bones is not a task for everyone, but Thatcher is willing to try. "You know, foreign sales are usually made by what we call a letter of credit. Let's say that we're selling something abroad—wheat to Russia, for example. Now the Russians will pay for that wheat only when they get control of it. The seller of the wheat—that's Stringfellow & Son (grain brokers) in this instance—wants to get paid as soon as it hands over the wheat."

Thatcher goes on to explain that the Russians have a bank account in London, and the London bank has an account in New York at the Sloan. When the wheat seller—Stringfellow & Son—presents the Sloan with the loading documents (the bill of lading) that prove he has handed over his wheat to the Russian ship, the Sloan pays him. Later the London bank pays the Sloan from the Russian account. That's the entire transaction.

"And the loading documents presented to you by Stringfellow & Son were your forged check?" asks the inspector.

"That's it exactly. When you're shipping wheat, the steamship gives you a bill of lading after the wheat is safely aboard—and that bill of lading is what Stringfellow brings to the bank. We pay, and in the normal course of events we send the bill of lading to London and they pay us. Unfortunately—"

Unfortunately the bill of lading handed over to Victor Quentin, head of the Sloan's Commercial Deposits Division, was the first ever from one of the Russian ships carrying US grain to Europe. Written in a combination of Russian and English, it looked like the real thing. Stringfellow's office had phoned Quentin to alert him to the fact that the documents would be arriving by messenger; Quentin was to send the Sloan check to Stringfellow at the Registry of Deeds.

To Quentin the papers looked authentic up to and including a special seal from the Russian trade office. He passed them and made out the check and sent it to the Registry of Deeds by Gus Denger, the driver of a rented limousine out of a livery called Halloran's Garage. All this occurred a week before the scene in Thatcher's office with Detective Inspector Lyons.

Only an hour before Lyons's arrival, Stringfellow called to say that he had just delivered the grain to the Russian ship, *Odessa Queen*, and would be sending a bill of lading to Sloan. Would the bank have ready his check for $985,000? At this point, after a quick check-up, it became obvious that the first bill of lading was a fake and the check—and the money—had gone to the wrong people.

Once Lyons has the story, he begins to plan his moves. He knows you can't fight city hall, conjures up images of senators, the FBI, the CIA, underfoot, hamstringing the investigation. And all because it's an international transaction. He rises and begins to act.

"All right, Mr. Thatcher. Let's talk to the chauffeur first."

Thatcher, Quentin, and Lyons repair to Halloran's Garage, where Rita Halloran, the owner, explains her business set-up to them. She has taken over the garage after the death of her husband, and has built it up from a car-hire deal to a respectable hire-lease business.

"Gus Denger drove one of our limousines. But we have a contract with Abe Baranoff to supply him with a car and driver whenever he's in town." She explains that Baranoff is a Russian who deals in real estate and motion pictures. "When he's in New York [Baranoff] has the exclusive use of a Caddie and Gus Denger. The rest of the time Gus is available for other jobs."

The three question Denger about his activities on the day he brought the documents to the Sloan and picked up the check. The details are as follows:

Baranoff was sailing that day for Russia on the *Queen Mary*. Gus drove him, his secretary, and his aides to the pier at 10 A.M. It is obvious from Denger's tone that he holds Baranoff, a high-rolling politico, in some contempt. After depositing the Russians at the *Queen Mary*, Denger returned to the garage, where he found a message from Baranoff's office. A woman had telephoned to say that Baranoff left some things at the pier for Denger to deliver elsewhere, but forgot to tell Denger. Returning to the pier, Denger received an envelope addressed to Victor Quentin at the Sloan. He drove to the bank with it.

When Quentin checked the documents, he noticed that Denger's next delivery was to the Registry of Deeds. He asked if Denger would mind taking along an envelope addressed to Luke Stringfellow there. Denger left the office with Sloan's check for $985,000 for Luke Stringfellow, went to the Registry of Deeds where a "medium-sized man with glasses, a hat and dark hair showing beneath it" identified himself as Luke Stringfellow and took the envelope.

"This girl who called," Thatcher asks. "Would you recognize her voice?" Denger corrects Thatcher, pointing out that he didn't take the call; a message was waiting for him at the garage. Mrs. Halloran says she may have received the message, but neglected to secure proper identification. "I get hundreds of similar calls from girls in offices all day long. Not a chance in a million I'd recognize the voice."

A new check is made out to Luke Stringfellow by the Sloan, the views of the State Department and the United States government having been duly delivered to Thatcher and the bank's chairman concerning the matter of honoring Luke Stringfellow's bona fide draft in order not to rock the boat of American–Russian trade relations.

As discreetly as possible Thatcher sets out to see if he and Quentin can discover how the *Odessa Queen*'s documents were faked. On the ride to the pier, the two discuss Denger, who seems to them to be terribly pleased with himself, as if he is enjoying a secret joke on all of them.

Commander Richardson of the US Navy Department joins them as they are welcomed aboard the Russian ship with a flurry of salutes. In the captain's cabin a huge red-faced Russian naval officer welcomes them. Three other Russians are present: a vivacious young woman translator whom any student of women, Thatcher notes, would consider a notable example of the breed; a Mr. Liputin, from Russia's Washington embassy; and a Mr. Voronin, a younger man with "assistant" written all over him, from the Russian consulate in New York. Commander Richardson knows some Russian, and the pretty translator is fluent in both tongues, as is the man from the consulate.

> Ominous glasses of colorless liquid appeared, thrust into the hands of the assemblage by the Captain, who was bellowing something high-spirited. Four rounds of vodka later, these facts had been agreed upon by all parties.

The *Odessa Queen* has nothing to do with this crime. Captain Kurnatovsky is a simple sailor and the Soviet people are friends of the American people. More vodka. Much clinking of glasses.

Thatcher tries to find out how bills of lading are handled on the *Odessa Queen*. None of the Russians understand the words "bill of lading." Finally Voronin, who is sitting a trifle outside the circle, unleashes a flood of Russian on Liputin, and after a few minutes of rising foreign voices, the interpreter tells Thatcher:

"The details you desire are obtainable at the consulate offices. Mr. Voronin suggests that you make an appointment to speak to

Sergei Durnovo there. He regrets that he himself must leave now. He extends to you his best wishes in your inquiry." Thatcher watches Voronin go, knowing that he is the only man likely to provide them with any information.

Thatcher, Quentin, and Richardson leave. Thatcher and Quentin take a cab uptown to the Russian consulate to see Durnovo.

There is a crowd controlled by police in front of the combination consulate and trade offices. Ukrainian pickets are waving placards. Thatcher and Quentin recognize Detective Inspector Lyons in charge. Just inside the door of the consulate a body is spread-eagled, face down, in a pool of blood. Lyons bends down, turns over the body: Gus Denger.

In addition to the theft of almost a million dollars from the Sloan, Thatcher is now faced with the problem of Gus Denger's murder. The American and Russian press view these events with the alarm one would expect.

Thatcher drives next to the office of Stringfellow & Son, where he meets Luke Stringfellow, a hale, hearty, and huge redheaded man and his female assistant, Tess Curtis, who handles all the details of the office. Thatcher elicits from them the information that it would be relatively easy to steal Stringfellow's letterheads from the front office of the receptionist, who often leaves her desk during the work day. Any steady visitor to the offices and anyone knowing that Stringfellow was involved with the Russian grain deal (including most banks, grain brokers, shipping lines and all of the Russian and American nationals party to the grain deal) would have access to company forms.

Thatcher decides he'll talk with the captain of the *Odessa Queen* again, but is informed by Stringfellow that the boat has sailed for Russia.

Instead, Stringfellow introduces Thatcher to Dave Yates, a friend and colleague who has dropped into the office. Yates is an Ivy League type from Willard & Climpson. Willard & Climpson and Stringfellow and Son are the two single largest purchasers of American grain resold to the Russians.

Next stop for Thatcher is the Russian Consulate, where he speaks with Durnovo, the commercial consulate, who, after many introductions and formalities, finally admits that it might be possible to filch a few letterheads from the desks of the trading commission. Durnovo is a tall, slim young man, obviously going places, who does not affect the rumpled homespun look of most lower-echelon Russian officials. The stamps, Durnovo says, are another matter. Procedures have been tightened up, and the stamps are in the hands of just a few people—all of them Russians.

Back at the Sloan, George Lancer, the chairman, after extended consultation with his legal department, sees one small ray of hope. The Sloan might be able to pass off some of its loss onto the foreign bank representing the Soviet Union.

"My God," remonstrates an official voice on the long-distance line from Washington. "Do you want to play into the hands of the Chinese?"

Lancer, who occasionally writes articles on international events, hastily denies the implication. He is advised to stay in the realm of theory and leave the implementation to the professionals.

Victor Quentin finally manages to trace the check for $985,000 when it comes in for payment. It was paid into a Puerto Rican bank and the funds immediately withdrawn to buy Mexican bearer bonds. Should he go further?

"No, no!" shrieks a voice from Washington. Any attempt to interfere with the liquidity or anonymity of Mexican bearer bonds will be seen by the Organization of American States as provocation and will constitute a death blow for the Alliance for Progress. "Do you want to play right into the hands of Castro?"

At this point a younger Sloan employee, MacDonald, discovers that the Sloan's insurance policy with Lloyd's of London just might cover the Sloan's loss. Should he proceed?

"Do you know what you're doing?" a voice sternly inquires. "Do you know there's a by-election coming up in England? It will center largely on the question of the future of NATO. Do you want to play into the hands of DeGaulle?"

But officialdom in Washington is not content to stymie all the Sloan's efforts toward recovery of the funds; it insists on reporting to the Sloan the results of its own efforts.

The CIA assures the Sloan that the whole caper is not a Communist Government plot. The FBI tells the Sloan that while they still look for Communists under every bed, Communism isn't a simple matter; it's America's New Left that is, and that's where the FBI is concentrating its big guns. The IRS finds no ties between Sloan's loss and the Mafia. And as if the Sloan doesn't have a kitful of troubles, Congress weighs in with a warning that it may trot out its own specialty—a Congressional investigation.

A higher-up envoy arrives from Russia to work with Thatcher on the case. The two discover, among other items:

- That David Yates, engaged to a wealthy New Yorker, has been seen hand-holding with the pretty Russian translator.
- That Baranoff has returned to the United States, now with a troupe of performing otters.
- That Luke Stringfellow has been involved in a land-purchase deal with Baranoff.

Thatcher and the Russian envoy realize that the scam was of necessity performed by *two* people: one well connected to the Russian trade commission and the other someone with access to the Stringfellow letterheads—not necessarily an American. Both must know the details of the grain deal.

How Thatcher figures out which American and which Russian are involved in the theft and the murder makes for the solution of this ingenious case.

In Lathen books women are sometimes heroines and sometimes villainesses, as Carr points out in *The Craft of Crime*. But they are not treated in the way that some of the more strident feminist writers handle them. Sex is handled in Lathen books in a genteel nineteenth-century way and is all the more effective for that treatment. Lathen writes of love and sex with great economy; each is therefore more exciting when encountered serendipitously in her works.

Literacy and civility are attributes common to the Lathen oeuvre. Said Latsis in the Carr interview: "We have reintroduced the colon, the semicolon, and the exclamation mark to the American reading public."[5]

Added Hennisart, "We were able to reintroduce the complex

sentence. It seems to me that the simple scheme of subject-verb-object has reigned long enough."

To which one can only add that in a Lathen book all the subjects have predicates. And every Lathen book is intricately and guilefully plotted and is, in addition, composed of very funny material.

9

Margaret Millar
The Evil Within

"Neuropaths pilot psychopaths along the labyrinthine ways of her narratives, and menace haunts her prose," said writer Aaron Marc Stein in his introduction of Margaret Millar at the 1983 MWA's Edgar Awards, where the lady was presented with the organization's Grand Master Award for a body of work dating back to 1941.

The award joins an Edgar won for her 1955 novel, *Beast in View*, and a 1965 Woman of the Year Award from the *Los Angeles Times* for her "outstanding achievements as a writer and a citizen."

"Mrs. Millar has created addicts rather than fans," said Dilys Winn in her book, *Murderess Ink*. "When her new hardcover comes out, they rush home to devour it. Dinner can wait. The dog can wait. They tell friends they'll call them back. That book gets finished in one sitting. And quoted from for months after. There has always been a bite to her work, an ability to nail a character so deftly, you think: Boy, I'm glad I'm not *her* enemy."[1]

Many mystery fans feel that Mrs. Millar is at least as talented if not more talented than her late husband, Kenneth, who published under the pseudonym Ross Macdonald. Ken Millar died in the summer of 1983. The Millars were married in 1938. Until his death, they had written happily at each other's side in their Santa Barbara home since the end of World War II.

Margaret Sturm was born in Kitchener, Ontario, Canada, in 1915. Her father was the mayor of the town. She started writing when she was eight. Her first story concerned four sisters who were three months apart in age. "I was sixteen before I found out why everyone thought that was hilarious." During her school days, she met Kenneth Millar, who was born in California but who moved to Canada with his parents when he was an infant. His parents soon separated.

After school in Kitchener, Margaret and Ken went to the University of Western Ontario, where they were married. Upon graduation, the Millars moved to Ann Arbor, Michigan, where Ken earned his Ph.D. at the University of Michigan. He taught at the university before serving in the navy in World War II.

While her husband was in the service, Margaret settled in Santa Barbara, California. In 1941, confined to her bed with a heart ailment, she read mysteries voraciously, then, against doctor's orders, wrote a detective novel (*The Invisible Worm*). It was moderately successful. Encouraged, she wrote two more in 1942 (*The Weak-eyed Bat* and *The Devil Loves Me*). All three feature a tall, whimsical psychiatrist-detective, Paul Prye.

(Her interest in mysteries piqued her husband's; his detective Lew Archer appeared first in 1949. Unwilling to trade in on his wife's name, his first books appeared under the name John Ross Macdonald; the pseudonym was shortened to Ross Macdonald when mystery writer John D. MacDonald began selling in a big way.)

Following *The Iron Gates*, Mrs. Millar wrote three nonmystery novels, *Experiment in Springtime* (1947), *It's All in the Family* (1948), and *The Cannibal Heart* (1949). "The only time I got on the bestseller list was with *It's All in the Family*, an autobiographical sort of thing," she said in a telephone interview in 1983.

Millar's mysteries continued to receive favorable reviews. *Rose's Last Summer* (1952) was made into a Hitchcock motion picture starring Mary Astor. Warner Brothers bought *The Iron Gates* as a starring vehicle for Bette Davis, but, as Mrs. Millar says, "the heroine died halfway through the book, and they couldn't get Bette Davis to agree to die—so they never made the movie."

Beast in View won the Edgar as best mystery novel of 1955.

The Millars were aware of California's natural beauty, and became alarmed at the spoilage of the state's air and water. The two of them founded a chapter of the National Audubon Society; the state's environmental and social phenomena are often evident in her books. *Beyond This Point Are Monsters* demonstrates her awareness of the problems between Anglos and Chicanos living in Southern California.

In *A Stranger in My Grave* (1960), Millar introduced Detective Steve Pinata; recently, in *Ask for Me Tomorrow* (1976) and *The Murder of Miranda* (1979) she has featured a young lawyer protagonist, Tom Aragon.

Between those two books came a serious illness, in which she underwent surgery for lung cancer. *Miranda* was finished while she had an uncomfortable attack of the shingles. The book, however, is light-hearted, even funny, and takes place around the beach club to which the Millars belonged for years.

The Millars had one child, a daughter, who died in 1970. After her husband died of Alzheimer's Disease, Mrs. Millar moved to a condominium close to the beach club, where she now lives with her dog, Misty.

When I spoke with her on the phone during the winter of 1984 she told me she was working on another book. "It's the only thing that keeps me sane since Ken's death."

Mrs. Millar is visually handicapped. Of her loss of vision she says, "Suddenly I just woke up one morning and things looked funny. First one eye went, then the other. It's a very strange disease, but I just have to roll with the punches."

How does she work?

"Well, I learned to type when I was young, so when the loss of vision happened, I simply began typing my books. A professional typist goes over it all when I finish. I also have a closed-circuit television set which projects what I write onto a 19-inch screen; I can see the enlarged text somewhat."

"Do you write about real people?" I asked.

"I never write about real people. Real people are duller than my people. I try to make my characters fun. Mine is a seriocomic style. I do see humor in the most tragic things, and vice versa."

She misses Ken's advice about her writing. "He was a critic before he became a writer and he was a great help to me. He was even his own editor at Knopf. After his death, I got hundreds of letters from people whom he actively edited, people whom he helped."

About the process of writing: "I often spend a day on a sentence. Some days, I'll write a sentence ten times. If I knew a lot of mystery writers who did that, then I think I'd read more of them. I can't stand sloppy writing and sloppy structure. I miss some of the older writers like Charlotte Armstrong and Helen McCloy.

"Sometimes I've worked as long as seven years on a book. I'd read what I'd written and say, '*That's* no good!' On the other hand, there've been the books that almost write themselves!"

In addition to her novels, Millar has published many short stories, which, according to her, have been "published and republished and republished."

In dealing with the psychopathology of crime, Mrs. Millar weaves her web and holds up her mirror to madness with infinite care. Her silences speak as eloquently as her words. She has been creating this magic for many years. Her nearest lineal descendant among the newer crime writers is Britain's Ruth Rendell.

It is interesting to note (perhaps coincidentally) the way in which Rendell's titles parallel titles of earlier Millar books: There is Millar's award-winning *Beast in View*, about a paranoid schizophrenic woman; and there is Rendell's *A Demon in My View*, which won Britain's Gold Dagger award, about a paranoid schizophrenic man. *The Devil Loves Me* was one of Millar's earliest books; Rendell's *Make Death Love Me* is of more recent vintage.

These (both Millar's and Rendell's books) are skillful studies in the broken pathways of the psyche and bear about as much resemblance to those one-dimensional books (in which a seemingly sane person is suddenly designated on the next-to-last page as a nut case who committed the crime) as gold resembles dross.

Rendell's writings, however, are relentlessly evil. Millar's are leavened with a pocketful of wry. Her collection of crazies range from the truly demonic to the gently daft. One of her most daft—and most engaging—is the elder Mrs. Osborne in *Beyond This Point Are Monsters*.

Beyond This Point Are Monsters

Devon Osborne, twenty-three, awakens on a hot October morning. Today is the day she is scheduled to go to court in San Diego and have her husband Robert declared legally dead. He has been gone for a year. His convertible with the keys in it is still parked in the garage. He went out after dinner to look for his dog one night and never returned.

Later, the dog was found dead on the highway, killed by a car. There were signs of a fight in the ranch worker's bunkhouse (bloodstains on the floor), but no one—not the workers, nor the ancient Chinese cook who served the workers—admitted to seeing or hearing anything. Ten migrant workers there at the time left in their truck before morning, but proved to be untraceable; they must have used false names and false immigration documents, only ten of hordes who yearly do the same thing to get work in the United States.

Devon arises, looks out her bedroom window over the farm that she and Robert own. It is the peak of the growing season. Berries have been followed by tomatoes, which have been followed by melons. She notes the migrant workers who come and go over the Mexican border, governed by the crops as the ocean tides are governed by the sun and the moon. She never meets them. They are hired by Estivar, Robert's Chicano foreman, who lives with his family in a small house on another part of the ranch, and who discourages her from communicating with the workers. Some speak English; those, Estivar says, are his San Diego cousins. The others speak Spanish and are Estivar's Mexican cousins.

Estivar, a lean, wiry man of fifty, was ranch supervisor under Robert's father, who founded the spread and died working it seven years before Robert's disappearance.

It is Mr. Ford, Robert's lawyer, who has persuaded Devon to petition the court to have Robert declared legally dead. Bills are piling up and cannot be paid without some legal determination as to Robert's circumstances.

She has fought this step for some time; then, one day recently, she simply packed up Robert's clothes, his tennis racquets, his trophies, his collection of silver coins, his maps, even his reading glasses, and marked them for delivery to the Salvation Army. Mrs. Agnes Osborne, Robert's mother, who moved from the ranch to a small house in San Diego when Devon and Robert married a year and a half ago, and who often drops in on Devon, offered to take the boxes to their destination. Mrs. Osborne is unreconciled to the fact that her only son is dead. Even after a year, even after offering a ten-thousand-dollar reward in the border towns and coming up empty, she continues to hope—that Robert has amnesia, or that he has been kidnapped and will return, walking in as casually as he walked out a year before.

Two cars head into the San Diego courthouse from the ranch.

Devon is driven in by Leo Bishop, her friend and the rancher whose property adjoins the Osborne ranch. Shortly before Robert brought her here as a bride from the East, Devon knows, Leo's wife, Ruth, drowned in the river separating the two ranches. Devon knows that Mrs. Osborne feels something is going on between Devon and Leo, just as there were rumors about Robert and Leo's wife years before.

The second car is driven by Estivar and carries his wife, Dulzura (Estivar's Mexican cousin and cook for the Osborne family), and Lum Wing (the elderly Chinese who cooks for the workers and lives in their bunkhouse). Jamie, fourteen, Estivar's youngest son (the three older ones have left the ranch) lies in the back of the station wagon, feeling important. He is to testify about finding a knife in the field three weeks after Robert's disappearance. He has shown the knife, with blood stains on it, to his father. Together with the torn sleeve of a plaid shirt found on a yucca bush outside the workers' bunkhouse with three different types of bloodstains on it, the knife constitutes the only concrete evidence that Robert may have died of foul play.

Mrs. Osborne watches Devon enter the courthouse. "She's such a mousy little thing." When Mrs. Osborne sent Robert away from the ranch after Ruth Bishop's death from drowning in the river she thought that the scandal would blow over. Instead Robert returned, at twenty-three, married to this Eastern college girl. Devon got pregnant, but after Robert's disappearance, lost the baby—and there went Mrs. Osborne's chances for a grandson and heir. But never mind; she *knows* Robert isn't dead. She took all those things Devon was giving to the Salvation Army, and re-created his room for Robert, awaiting his return. She even pinned to the door of his room an ancient map that said at its borders: "Beyond This Point Are Monsters."

She plans to offer another reward for information about Robert's whereabouts; and this time she will make sure it is circulated even more widely than the first one.

> In the Matter of the Estate of Robert Kirkpatrick Osborne, Deceased, the petition of Devon Suellen Osborne respectfully shows:
>
> That she is the surviving wife of Robert Osborne.
>
> That Petitioner is informed and believes and upon such information and belief alleges that Robert Osborne is dead.
>
> The precise time of his death is not known but Petitioner believes and therefore alleges that Robert Osborne died on the thirteenth day of October, 1967.
>
> The Petitioner and her husband, Robert Osborne, lived together as husband and wife for approximately half a year. On the evening of October 13th, Robert Osborne, after dining with his wife, left the ranch house to look for his dog which had wandered off in the course of the afternoon. When Robert Osborne failed to return by half past nine Mrs. Robert Osborne roused the foreman of the ranch and a search was organized. It was the first of many such searches covering a period of months and an area of hundreds of square miles. Evidence has been collected which proves beyond a reasonable doubt that between 8:30 and 9:30 on the night of October 13, 1967, Robert Osborne met his death at the hands of two or more persons.

In the corridors outside the courtroom, a pretty Mexican girl speaks to Devon. "You remember me, Mrs. Osborne. Carla? I took care of the Estivar twins two summers ago. Valenzuela, the cop, must have it in for me. I got subpoenaed."

Devon scarcely remembers the girl hired by Estivar to care for the Estivar infant twins—a pair of girls after four Estivar sons. She was sent away by Estivar's wife, who didn't like the way Carla twitched her miniskirt at the three oldest Estivar sons, Cruz, Rufo, and Felipe. Rufo is now married, Cruz is in the army, and Felipe is rumored to be working in Seattle.

"Your name is Secundo Alvino Juan Estivar?"

"Yes."

"You are foreman of the Osborne ranch?"

"Yes." Estivar shifts in his chair. "When the ranch makes money, I don't take the credit. When there's a robbery and a murder I'm not taking the blame!"

The lawyer says, "Nobody's blaming you."

"Not in words. But I can smell it a mile away. I hire people in good faith. If it turns out their names and addresses are phoney and their papers forged, it's not my fault."

"Kindly simmer down, Mr. Estivar. Tell us when you first arrived at the ranch."

"In 1943, from Sonora, Mexico."

Estivar has worked on the ranch since before Robert was born. Robert's father, Estivar says, was a hard drinker. Robert played with Estivar's sons as they grew up. The summer he was fifteen, Robert began going over to the Osborne ranch, to see Leo and Ruth. They gave him a puppy. That summer, Mr. Osborne was killed in a farming accident, and Mrs. Osborne sent Robert off to prep school.

"When he returned he wasn't a kid anymore. He was the boss."

"Would you say there was mutual respect between you?"

"No, sir. Mutual interest. Mr. Osborne had no respect for me and my family any more. It was that school she sent him to. He learned prejudice there. I'd learned to live with it, but how could I explain to my sons that the Robbie they played with didn't exist any more?"

"What happened last September at the ranch?"

Estivar tells the attorney that a lot has happened at the ranch—all of it bad. There was a grape strike on. Estivar's second son, Rufo, got married, moved out, and went to live in Salinas. His third son, Felipe, left to try to find employment in some other field. Only Cruz, Estivar's elder son, stayed to help his father—and they were putting in sixteen-hour days until the old truck arrived with ten workers in it. Estivar hired them as soon as they could pile out of their truck.

He testifies that on the night of October 13, he heard their truck go into town and return about nine. The next morning all ten men were gone in the truck. So was Robert.

Lum Wing, who slept in the bunkhouse in a corner curtained off from the workers, describes a fight among one or two Mexicans and Robert Osborne. No one knows how much English or Spanish Lum Wing can understand. "I mind my own business, I hear fight, I put in earplugs. I sleep innocent as a babe until Mr. Estivar wakes me. And he says what has happened is: there is blood all over the floor and Mr. Osborne is missing."

Valenzuela, the police officer on duty at the time of the alleged murder, testifies that the bunkhouse floor was covered with blood, that he discovered the shirt sleeve outside the bunkhouse with three types of blood on it.

And that let him to believe—?

"That there was a fight between three people in the bunkhouses, since there were three different blood types involved. One type, AB negative, was the same type as Robert Osborne was known to have."

Agnes Osborne has driven to her house after the morning session in court and decides not to return to the ranch. The way that Estivar blackened the names of her husband and son! Such ingratitude!

At the time of Robert's disappearance, Valenzuela said he thought Robert had been taken into Mexico or perhaps "dumped into the sea." It was Valenzuela, now retired from the police force and selling insurance, who took around Agnes Osborne's reward circulars. She now decides to contact him again to distribute a new circular offering a larger reward.

Leo and Devon lunch together. "Robert would come over to our house when things got rough," Leo tells her. "Old Mr. Osborne drank and his wife couldn't admit it. He'd be carried from the fields, and she'd talk about his migraine—that, and bang out hymns on her piano. 'Onward Christian Soldiers!'"

When Mrs. Osborne doesn't return to court, Devon drives to her house and knocks on the door. There is no answer. She enters the house, and finds a note on the table. It contains some sentences in Spanish and English.

> The sum of $10,000 will be paid to anyone furnishing information—

Devon walks through the house. On the door to the front bedroom is the map and a sign: "Beyond This Point Are Monsters." It was in the boxes of junk designated for the Salvation Army. In the room Devon finds a shrine to the young Robert. Mrs. Osborne has never intended to give his things away.

In the other bedroom lies Mrs. Osborne. She won't testify *that* afternoon; she is drugged on sleeping pills.

Devon returns to the court and the court declares Robert legally dead.

Old Mrs. Osborne goes on with her own plans. She offers a new reward for information about Robert, seeing to it that the posters are circulated in all the border towns. Then she sets about awaiting the phone call that will tell her about Robert.

Finally, the telephone call comes, and Mrs. Osborne sets about discovering what happened to Robert.

As the book unfolds, it does so on two separate levels, each beautifully developed by Millar. The first level is the disappearance of Robert Osborne in the previous year. The second level is the story of the Osbornes and the Estivars, two families bound together rather more closely than Estivar has stated on the stand: that the two men shared mutual interest but not mutual respect. The relationship of an Anglo ranch family whose prosperity is tied to that of the family of the Chicano ranch foreman is an exercise in symbiosis. The families will survive, even if one or two of their individual members do not.

10

Shannon OCork

The Blood Sports

Shannon OCork, with a name out of a novel and a look that's in the tradition of the beautiful blondes who decorate the pages of Dashiell Hammett or John D. MacDonald, came to mystery writing from previous careers in theater and sports photography. She scored a solid hit with *Sports Freak*, her first book about the adventures of a second-string female sports photographer sleuth and is the first to credit a "money" review from "Newgate Callendar" in the *New York Times Book Review* for its success. Still under forty years of age, OCork is turning T. T. Baldwin's adventures into a cable television series.

When I interviewed OCork, in Guilford, Connecticut, in July, 1983, her third book, *Hell Bent for Heaven* (St. Martin's Press) had just received a flattering review in the prestigious *New Yorker Magazine*.

"That pleased me," she said, looking out over Long Island Sound. "I've often sent pieces to *The New Yorker*, at first getting printed rejection slips, then rather nice little letters saying, 'This is not right; try us again.' A favorable review in that magazine was more than just a review to me.

"I was born on a Kentucky farm. Back there, where I dreamed of being the kind of person I still hope to become I yearned to be printed in *The New Yorker*. It seemed to be the most wonderful magazine in the world—everyone in it was bright and lovely and good-spirited and well-dressed and having fun and being social and having friends who were also delightful.

"On the farm I had a mother who was busy being a nurse and a father who was busy being a failure and I spent a lot of time with an older sister who seemed a bit of an ogre at the time. She tyrannized me and her tyranny revolved around words! She'd give me words to spell and pronounce—like bouquet—and if I missed the spelling or the pronunciation she'd chain me to a tree or take me to the barn and drop hay balls on my head, telling me they were spiders. My favorite companions were really the dogs and horses and books."

OCork leaned back in the deck chair and sipped a glass of Chablis. "My father died when I was sixteen. I had just been graduated from high school. I worked all summer long at the local White Castle hamburger place and saved almost a thousand dollars. I was going to New York to become a writer. I bade farewell to the farm and my mother, bought an old Hudson auto for a hundred dollars, and headed for New York with my little Royal portable.

"I arrived in the fall, and was able to rent for the winter a summer bungalow in Far Rockaway. It was right on the beach. I bought two portable heaters, and I lived for a hundred dollars a month there, waiting on tables as I wrote my novel. I would go down to the sea at low tide and dig for clams. I bought black bread and butter. I thought that God was giving me food, and life was being very good to me.

"When the book was finished I sent it to Random House. They wrote me back a nice letter; they asked for changes. *Now* I understand; at the time I thought they had rejected the book. I took it at high tide into the ocean and tore it up and threw it away. I thought, 'I'm a failure as a writer. What is there left for me?'

"I hurt." She closed her eyes at the memory.

"But if you are bright enough—and poor enough—New York State will, after the taking and passing of certain tests, send you to college. I had never thought of going to college when I was little. My father had said, 'You go to work and get a job,' while my mother counseled me, 'If you want to be an artist you must marry a rich man.' She would introduce me to doctors. But I wasn't really a 'doctor' person; I wasn't clingy or ultrafeminine.

"I enrolled at Hofstra University in Hempstead, New York, on scholarship. I was a theater major; I wrote plays that were done in the school's workshop. I got married while I attended college; he was a fledgling writer, too.

"When we graduated I went into a doctoral program at Tufts University near Boston, again as a theater major. I acted, directed—but I still yearned to write. I was supposed to go to London to study for a year, but my husband, who feared that if I went to England I'd never return to him, said, 'What can I give you that will make you *not* miss a year in London and a Ph.D?'

"I thought about it, and said 'my own theater.' And he did it! He found a big, old warehouse, rented it, stripped it, put up lights and platforms—all on the cheap—but gave me a theater called the Craft Experimental Theatre in Kenmore Square, Boston, where I produced and directed plays and made a bit of a reputation for myself. It lasted three years, but when my marriage fell apart, I sold the theater and came back to New York, determined to do what I'd done ten years before—become a writer in New York City.

"I had an Actor's Equity card, and I began writing articles for the Equity publication. They couldn't pay me anything for the stories, but they said 'If you take pictures for your articles we'll pay you fifteen dollars for each one.' I got hold of a camera, began experimenting with it and soon I was earning fifteen dollars a shot for my Equity photographs."

She paused to watch a gull wheeling and shrieking overhead.

"About that time I met a man who was a sports fan. He'd take me to ball games, to the fights at Madison Square Garden. I began taking photographs at the fights and got kind of good at it. I sold some photographs to *Ring Magazine*, the boxer's bible. Soon the magazine hired me as a stringer. I became their first woman photographer, started doing their covers of title fights, began to write pieces for them (at a wondrous seventy-five dollars a throw!), while writing my first novel, *Sports Freak*.

"Sounds like a circuitous, tortuous route—and yet, it was all great fun! I never felt sorry for myself, never went on welfare, although my income ranged from thirty-five to forty-five hundred a year."

OCork took a course at Womanschool in New York City on

marketing her manuscript. "Couldn't interest an agent in it! Each said to me: 'You have written a category book. No sex. No violence. Not worth our time. Go sell it, and I'll arrange your contract.' So I began sending it around myself. Doubleday said 'No.' Simon & Schuster 'took it to the table'—meaning the editor liked it—but the editorial board said 'No.' I sent it to St. Martin's Press; it found a home there. No advertising, no promotion, one of many others. But Newgate Callendar of the *New York Times Book Review* read it and gave it a marvelous review which turned my career around. I don't know who he is but I sent him a red rose. Hope he got it!

"After that the agent Julian Bach began handling my work."

Sports Freak, which has a pro football background and is set in upstate New York, was picked up by a Canadian film company. The hardcover edition sold out and Pocket Books published the reprint in softcover form.

"I was lucky," OCork continued. "I mean that. No one is interested at first, no matter how good you are. You just keep on, you know. With the advance from the book I went out and bought myself an IBM Selectric typewriter for a thousand dollars. My advance was three thousand.

"When *Freak* was optioned for the movies I went to Maximillian the furrier. I went into the salon in a ratty rabbit and I came out in a seven-thousand-dollar mink. They were very nice to me. They looked at my rabbit, then had the model show me all their coats. I paid for mine by check. They took me into a very pretty room, and they gave me tea and a bisquit—a fat little cookie—and they said 'Now we're going to put your fur in a very nice bag and wrap it for you,' but what they really were doing was phoning my bank to be sure my check wouldn't bounce. I loved them for it; they were doing it so nicely."

After the first novel moved so briskly, the publisher wanted another starring T. T., and then a third. The second (*End of the Line*) had a sports fishing background; the third (*Hell Bent for Heaven*), a rodeo background at Madison Square Garden.

"I wrote a mainstream novel about a band of evil bag women. I spent eighteen months on it and all of the remainder of the money I had earned from my first novel. And no one would buy it; every editor I sent it to hated it. In today's political atmosphere I guess people don't want to hear about the ragtags winning the war."

OCork still wants to try other fiction avenues—a novel of romantic suspense, for example. "If T. T. Baldwin becomes a series television character, I still don't want to be trapped in it. Agatha Christie got trapped in one series character—Poirot—then another—Miss Marple—and yet a third—Tommy and Tuppense. I don't want that to happen to me. But I'm having fun. In a sense I've done what I set out to do."

Indeed.

The lady is on a roll! Earlier in the summer of 1983, OCork married Hillary Waugh, veteran mystery writer and former executive vice president of the Mystery Writers of America. Gregory MacDonald (creator of the Fletch detective series) gave the bride away. The ceremony was held in front of the couple's house in Guilford, Connecticut, overlooking Long Island Sound. The house is amicably partitioned: the groom writes his police procedurals in a corner of the living room. OCork's Selectric and her files are on a screened porch. First order of business after the honeymoon was turning the three novels about T. T. Baldwin into screen treatments for the possible cable television series.

Sports Freak

Sports Freak, the first novel in the series written by OCork, introduces T. T. (for Theresa Tracy) Baldwin, female sports photographer, second-string, for the tabloid newspaper, the *New York Graphic*. T. T. is blonde and bright, in her midtwenties and has one of the fastest mouths in the East. (OCork has a good ear for New York speech patterns.) "T. T. is busy, ambitious, talented, a bit cynical and very nosy, pushy when necessary, making her way in the world, doing what she loves to do and doing it very well," according to *New York Times* mystery reviewer Newgate Callendar.[1]

The only woman in the twin male sanctuaries of newspapers and sports, T. T. contends with general male prejudice and resentment and with the particular niggling and naggling of her senior male colleague and partner, Floyd Beesom, master of the action shot and double scotches. She does so with good spirits.

T. T. is a talented photographer, in love with her cameras, bright and ambitious. Her ability, her drive, and her sense of humor are her saving graces at the *Graphic*—newspapermen understand ambition, demand competence and are always suckers for a good laugh line.

Floyd Beesom, the Graphic's premier sports photographer, is T. T.'s sometime partner and always rival. Floyd is a redoubtable, hard-boozing master of the action shot, and he thinks T. T. should be photographing hemlines instead of third downs.

In uneasy partnership, along with Gilbert (Gilly Fats—only not to his face) Ott, senior sports writer who "can write the best copy with the thinnest material of anybody on the sports staff and frequently does," T. T. and Floyd are sent by the managing editor of the *Graphic* to the affluent upstate New York town of High Mountain for the opening of the football season—the opening game of two new NFL franchises, the High Mountain Climbers (the home team) and the Coastville Johnny Rebs. The game takes place in High Mountain's new sports complex, the Colossus, and features the professional debut of the NFL's newest highest-paid contract player, former star quarterback for Penn State, Lovable Lou LaMont. The owner of the High Mountain Climbers is an elegant elderly widow, Mrs. Marcella Snowfield, rich and rabid football fan.

Seven minutes into the game, star rookie quarterback LaMont is head-butted by seasoned dirty-tricks player Billy "The Badman" O'Leary of the Johnny Rebs. Knocked unconscious, LaMont is later pronounced dead by the attending team physician, Dr. José ("Call Me Joe") DeBianco.

Only T. T. Baldwin gets the shots of the particular "killing" play. (Floyd Beesom was busy photographing a cheerleader's air splits from underneath with his zoom lens.)

The murder weapon turns out to be an acupuncture needle deep in the base of Lovable Lou's brain, under his Climbers helmet, hidden in his thick black coiffured curls. But how did the needle get there, to be driven to the point of death during the rough-and-tumble of the game?

T. T. follows the stretcher-borne LaMont into the locker room. On the path she is stopped by one of the Climber's cheerleaders (they're called, collectively, The Scenic View), who calls to T. T. to "ask about the needle," and then disappears.

Two uniformed policemen — Lieutenant Weatherwax and his subordinate, Detective John Xavier — are on the scene when Dr. DeBianco announces that LaMont is dead from major arterial collapse. He says he doesn't understand the cause of the collapse.

T. T. butts in. "Needles, Dr. Joe. Did you find any needles?"

DeBianco goes back to investigate the possibilities of needles and the two police officers look at her with amusement — until the doctor returns with an acupuncture needle in hand. The two officers try in vain to get T. T. to divulge the source of her information.

What should have been a victory party in the Colossus for the Climbers turns out to be a police interrogation. On the tables are peanuts and condiments for the hot dogs and hamburgers that are to be the dinner food — pickle relish, spicy French mustard, chopped raw onions. As T. T., Floyd, and Gilly Fats sit down at a table, the reader meets the remainder of the Climbers cadre. There are David and Babs Livingston — he is publicity director for the Climbers, she is a cheerleader — and they've been married four months. There are Amy Bland, High Mountain's Marilyn Monroe look-alike, and Rachel Hirshaw, only child of Abe Hirshaw, the Climbers' general manager. Amy and Rachel are both cheerleaders, with Rachel engaged to marry DeBianco, the team's doctor. Star of The Scenic View is Wanda Pettigo, and there is Patty Cambron, who told T. T. about the needle. There is Stanley, the janitor. And there is Lil Harv, who smells of cod-liver oil and who might be the most terrifying teenager of all time, traveling as he does at silent, lightning speed in a motorized wheelchair, smiling a pretty smile, a sort of team mascot adopted by the Climbers. There's Floyd, too.

T. T. goes to the bar to get drinks for Floyd and herself, and returns to find that Floyd has eaten one of her hot dogs — and gotten horribly, messily ill. DeBianco takes over, Floyd is rushed to the hospital, and everyone realizes he has been poisoned by something hidden in the mustard-slathered hot dog he sneaked off T. T.'s plate. T. T. resolves to solve the case, score a beat, and make a reputation for herself.

T. T.'s quest leads her into the private lives of the five cheerleaders, into the fancy digs of Mrs. Marcella Snowfield, into different bedrooms and difficult positions. OCork introduces the reader to some raunchy characters (DeBianco, who's into necrophila, and

Lil Harv's mother, who enjoys energetic and imaginative couplings).

T. T. finds the body of Patty Cambron stuffed into a locker in the cheerleaders' dressing room in the Colossus. She learns that Wanda, Patty's roommate, was sleeping with LaMont, got pregnant by him, and had an abortion. Back in Pennsylvania LaMont's father was a prison guard. During a prison riot, he shot a prisoner, leaving the convict emasculated. T. T. assumes that this may be a good enough reason for the victim to seek out the jailer's son for revenge. Which of the Climbers was imprisoned twelve long years before in Pennsylvania?

In the denouement, with Lil Harv riding his wheelchair like a Roman chariot during the filming of a television commercial for Vitamin E, the murderer is drilled by the chair and dies the way Lou LaMont did, an acupuncture needle through the brain.

"*Reportage*," writes OCork, "is, at best, a filtered truth, a mix of fact and fancy filtered through a writer."[2] She goes on, in a series of rules about writing: "It is the nature of truth to become muddy. Move away from truth as soon as you can into clean and beautiful lies. Ground your lies in little verifiable truths. This way you fool most of the people all of the time.

"I write about people and sports," says OCork. "I'm much more interested in character—and characters—than in putting a puzzle together, and in figuring out the patient, plodding methods used by police to solve crimes."

At one time a critic[3] put together a formula for writing a successful mystery story. It went:

½ Sherlock Holmes
¼ P. G. Wodehouse
¼ Something you know

OCork's T. T. Baldwin is a persistent, wily sleuth, and is wickedly funny. She knows more about football than Howard Cosell. So, seemingly, does OCork, whose prose about sports and athletes is almost Hemingwayesque in its muscular purity.

11

Ruth Rendell

Terror Times Two

"With twenty-two books written over eighteen years, Ruth Rendell has established a double eminence in two separate categories of crime fiction: the classic puzzle, with a stable background and a recurring cast headed by a mildly eccentric detective and his more conventional subordinate; and the novel of pure suspense, in which a blundering innocent and a haunted psychopath become fatally entangled in a paranoid atmosphere of cross purposes and sinister coincidence. . . . In both fields success is difficult . . . In the first, because it has been so thoroughly mined from Agatha Christie to P. D. James and the second, pioneered by the lone figure of Patricia Highsmith, is all the more daunting because comparatively unexplored. Ruth Rendell's remarkable talent has been able to accommodate the rigid rules of the reassuring mystery story as well as the wider range of the disturbing psychological thriller."[1]

With her two-tiered talent Rendell has become, according to the *Boston Sunday Globe*, "the best mystery writer . . . anywhere in the English-speaking world."[2] The number of awards garnered by this beautiful Englishwoman mounts yearly: Current Crime's silver cup for the best British crime novel of 1975 for *Shake Hands Forever*; the Crime Writers' Association's 1976 Gold Dagger for *A Demon in My View*; the 1980 Arts Council National Book Award in Genre Fiction for *The Lake of Darkness*. Her books have been translated into fourteen languages, and at the 1981 International

Congress of Crime Writers in Stockholm, Rendell received Sweden's award as the top crime writer of the year. In addition to the kudos received for her novels, Rendell has, in addition, received two Edgars from MWA for short stories that have appeared in *Ellery Queen's Mystery Magazine*. The first was for "The Fallen Curtain," the most recent, for her 1983 story, "The New Girlfriend."

At the dinner in Stockholm honoring the world's best crime writers, if Mary Higgins Clark in swirling black taffeta and twinkling gems, was the most glamorous attendee, Rendell, in her early fifties, as is Clark, was certainly the most chic. She has beautifully cut dark hair, with just a suggestion of silver winglets over each ear, and wore a black-and-gray harlequin-printed short chiffon frock.

Like P. D. James, Rendell never went to college.

"I've always been a great reader," she told me. "I must have read every English novel from *Beowulf* on, but I'm not a great mystery reader. I must have read Agatha Christie and Dorothy Sayers, but neither made a big impression on me."

Often compared to Christie because of her devious plots, Rendell much prefers to be compared to the American suspense writer Patricia Highsmith.

"I suppose I've been writing all my life," says Rendell. "I had had a lot of short stories rejected by various magazines before I wrote my first novel, which was accepted in 1964, when I was thirty-four."

Rendell, for years, lived in London and also in a small, thatched cottage in Sussex with her husband, Donald, and a son, who is a social worker. Recently the Rendells bought a five-hundred-year-old house located in a wood. Their son now lives in the cottage. The Rendells were, at one time, divorced, and then after four or five years, were remarried.

Kingsmarkham is the name of the murder-prone Sussex village policed by Chief Inspector Wexford and Inspector Burden in Rendell's fiction oeuvre. In the first Wexford book *From Doon with Death* (1964), Wexford was fifty-two years old. ("Wish I'd known how successful he'd be," comments Rendell. "I'd have made him about fifteen") He is a tall, ungainly, rather ugly man who was once fat but slimmed down for reasons of health. He is addicted to literary quotations, is happily married to the understanding Dora, has two daughters . . . and if he resembles any other detective today it is probably Georges Simenon's Maigret, whom Rendell admires. Burden is prim, handsome, and the proper foil for his superior, Wexford. Since 1964, this permanent cast of characters has changed and grown—yet each succeeding Kingsmarkham book is unique, so that a reader never feels he or she has missed something in reading the sixth, or the tenth, rather than beginning with the first and reading each one in sequence.

The non-Wexford books, however, are more complex with enough pathology to interest Freud.

"To read them is to delve into Krafft-Ebing territory. They're a bit on the kinky side, and guaranteed to disturb anybody who had planned on settling down with a Poirot figure for an hour or two."[3]

A pervasive awareness of impending disaster, a nightmare fantasy overlaid by a stolid realism—these are the staples of the Rendell suspense oeuvre.

Rendell hates one of her books, her third novel, *In Sickness and in Health*, about a thirty-eight-year-old protagonist who is pregnant and doesn't know it and who thinks her husband is trying to poison her. "It's a silly book, the protagonist is a stupid woman. I would never write that now." Still, one miss in a succession of hits. . . .

Rendell writes one book a year. "It takes me a year because I write everything three times. I write a draft, then I rewrite it. Then I do my own typing, and I am always changing things around as I type.

"I can't write to order. Not too long ago, to my humiliation and chagrin, I had a short story rejected by an English magazine because they had asked me to write it, they told me what they wanted, and I wrote what they asked me to write. I thought I was too marvelous ever to be rejected, which just goes to show how absolutely wrong I was."

So far only one Rendell book has been translated into a motion picture or television show. She remembers the movie as "a rather awful one—it never really got off the ground. It was definitely a 'B' picture." She has hopes of a Wexford television series. Her *Shake Hands Forever*, a Wexford story, has been optioned by the BBC. *A Judgement in Stone*, a psychological novel, has also been optioned.

She is startled by the kinds of money paid by American publishers and producers. "The way people throw enormous sums away without having any more care about it! Even if they never make the movie you do get quite a lot of money out of it."

Rendell has many American friends and comes often to this country. "I don't terribly like doing television and talk shows. It depends on how much you look upon writing as a business and how much you look upon it as something you like to do and you try to do well. I am not prepared to sacrifice myself to make a Roman circus for the possibility of selling another thousand dollars worth of books."

Currently, Rendell is far ahead of her writing schedule.

"We went on a visit to China, and when I returned I broke into a book I'd been working on to get a China story down right after I returned." (*Speaker of Mandarin*, an Inspector Wexford book, was published in the spring of 1984.) Her next book is about a strange London family.

Asked to name her first great success, the book which made her financially independant, Rendell hesitates.

"There never was such a time, really. I'd been publishing for ten years, when suddenly I received a Gold Dagger for *A Demon in My View*, which I guess was my first great success, and I'd been slowly building an audience . . . but it took a long time to build."

There is now, in addition to the novels, a reasonable market in women's magazines for mystery short stories, and Rendell writes these as well as her novels. She is very pleased with her new home.

"We are seven miles in Suffolk. The house is very old, located in a wood and I have three very nice cats. I shall certainly use it all in a setting in a future book."

A Demon in My View

"The cellar was divided into rooms. Each of these chasms except the last was cluttered with legless or armless chairs, broken bicycles . . . all this rubbish was coated with the grime that is always present in cellars.

"He came down the steps with the torch in his hand, to the last room. He played the torch; it showed him a woman's figure. Her white face, beautiful, unmarked by any flaw of skin or feature, shivered in the light.

"He didn't speak. He had never been known to talk to women. He put down his torch. Then he approached her, paralyzed as she was, and meeting no resistance, he closed his hands over her throat. His hands squeezed until the fingers met, and as forefinger met thumb, the beautiful face changed, caved in in agony. He gave a grunting gasp as her figure fell sideways. He released his hold, swaying at the earthquake inside him, and let her fall.

"It took him a few minutes to recover. He wiped his hands and the corners of his mouth on a clean handkerchief. Then he picked up the plastic shop window model and set her once more against the wall. Her face remained caved in. Inserting his finger through the split in her neck, a split which grew wider each time he murdered her, he pushed out the sunken nose and crumpled eyes until she was blank and beautiful again. She was ready to die for him again. A week, two weeks might go by, but she would wait for him, wait until next time."

Kenbourne Vale in London, which is the setting for this atmosphere of calmly described mayhem, is a series of houses that are warrens for people, little anthills of discomfort.

At 142 Trinity Road, the owner, Stanley Caspian, has come to collect the weekly rents from the tenant, Arthur Johnson. The two were friends at school. There are five flats in the building, where Arthur has lived since his Auntie Gracie died some twenty years before.

Stanley tells Arthur that a new tenant, Anthony Johnson, will be moving into room 2A. Stanley makes a joke about the two not getting their mail mixed up because of their similar last names. Arthur is not amused.

He takes his laundry to the laundromat, does his grocery shopping for the week, and returns to his flat on the top floor of 142 Trinity, where he dusts his cut glass, makes his bed with pink sheets, and thinks about the house he has now lived in for twenty years.

It was when he was redecorating as he moved in that he went to the cellar for a stepladder and chanced upon the dummy. Alone in the cellar, he advanced on the mannikin. So that was how clothing store dummies looked! With fear, with awe he looked at the two hemispheres on her chest. He had done so many secret things in his life that no inhibition intervened when he fetched from the flat one of Auntie Gracie's dresses, her handbag, her shoes. . . . Before he knew what he was doing he had strangled her. The release had been almost as good as the real thing. You do not have to hide or sweat for such a killing. The law permits you to kill anything not made of flesh and blood. He left her and went into the yard, the first of many such departures.

The room now number 2 was untenanted then. Only that room and his own flat look down on the cellar door.

Arthur knows that he is a perfectly normal man who just happens to have a small peculiarity he is well able to keep under control.

Next morning, the tenants are off to work: the Kotowsky couple, quarreling as usual; Jonathan Dean, soon to be leaving the house; Li-Li Chan, the Chinese girl, being picked up by a chap in a red convertible. Arthur does not approve of Li-Li. He checks through the mail, arranges it in neat piles on the front hall table, goes off to his own job as bookkeeper in a neighborhood plumbing-supply shop.

Anthony Johnson—tall, young, handsome—moves into 142 Trinity Road, with a large old suitcase and a canvas bag holding his works on sociology, psychology, his dictionary of psychology, and his texts on abnormal psychology. He has taken this room because of its proximity to the library of Radclyffe College, Kenbourne Vale. There he hopes to write his thesis on "Some Aspects of the Psychopathic Personality," which will secure for him from the University of London his doctorate in philosophy. He has worked with the poor, the sick, the deprived. He has never awakened to sexual awareness, however, until he met Helen and his soul's eye was turned towards the light.

Unfortunately for Anthony, Helen is married—to Roger, stupid, possessive, and unable to do anything but win pistol-shooting contests. What is it that Roger has that he, Anthony, lacks? To give Helen a chance to decide, Anthony has come to live in Kenbourne Vale.

The library is an advantage, of course, but his theory is that absence will make Helen's heart grow fonder—of him. Anthony can't write to her—Roger might intercept the letter. But she will write him once a week, and he will phone her on Roger's night out at pistol practice.

Anthony has given Helen a deadline. By November she must decide between them. She can stay in prison with Roger, or come out with Anthony into the free air.

A man of fifty in an immaculate gray suit, holding a bunch of grocery-store coupons in his hand, is standing by the hall table as Anthony comes down. Arthur jumps as he sees Anthony.

"These were on the mat," he tells Anthony. "You wouldn't think there was a world-wide paper shortage, would you?"

"I'm Anthony Johnson. I moved in today. Are you by any chance the other Johnson?"

Arthur gives a reproving laugh. "I think you must mean you are the other Johnson. I've been here for twenty years."

Every morning thereafter Arthur listens carefully for Anthony to go off to work. He is certain that Anthony remains home evenings. Arthur peers out his curtained window, sees the light in room 2 come on each evening about six and remain on. Anthony does not draw his curtains. It is a little early for Arthur to feel an urge to visit the cellar again; yet he is growing restless.

The first letter comes for Anthony Johnson. Arthur knows the letter is for Anthony because it is postmarked York and comes from a Mrs. R. L. Johnson, but the front is addressed ambiguously—to Mr. A. Johnson, Esq., 2/142 Trinity Road. Arthur is exasperated. He brings the letter to Anthony, points out to him the consequences of such imprecision. Anthony is casual about it. "Let's not meet trouble halfway. I won't get many letters, and the ones I get will either be postmarked York, from my mother, or Bristol."

"Very well. I thought I should mention it and I have. Now you can't blame me if there's any mix-up."

"I shan't blame you."

All the same, Arthur is irritated. When he takes the post Tuesday, he sets aside the letter from Bristol with no sender's name on it. When he returns to the house after work, the letter has disappeared.

That evening, Arthur hears Anthony mount the stairs to the landing where the pay phone is located. A lot of digits are dialed, coins are inserted, and presently Arthur hears:

"Had your letter, darling. I take it that the coast is clear, that he's not listening in on any extension, that he won't come here and shoot me in the morning? . . . go out in the evenings? Lovey, where would I go and who would I go with?"

Anthony becomes friendly with the other tenants, Jonathan and the Kotowskys, who are on the verge of separating. Tony tells them all about his thesis.

"You ought to become friendly with our own murderer, then," says Jonathan. The Kenbourne killer, he's called. Twenty-five years ago he strangled his first victim, Maureen Cowan. Five years later, he struck again; this time a student nurse, Bridget O'Neill, was the victim. The police never caught the killer of either girl.

When Jonathan Dean moves away, he is replaced by Linthea, an attractive West Indian girl with a small son. As they are putting their empty suitcases in the basement, the boy discovers the dummy in the back room and shows it to Linthea and Anthony.

It is now November. Helen writes to Anthony that she hasn't made up her mind between him and Roger as yet. Roger can't bear to be frozen out of her life; she says that she must wait until Christmas. Can't Anthony come to Bristol at Christmas?

Anthony now gives Helen a deadline on the phone: her next letter is her last chance. She must tell Anthony she is leaving Roger to come to him, or it's the end. When Anthony hangs up he calls Linthea in her apartment and asks her to join him in his room. She does.

Arthur watches them through his curtains.

It is Guy Fawkes Day, and the neighborhood children have gathered in the common to set fire to their huge Guy Fawkes bonfire, with the dummy of Fawkes hanging over it. Anthony is master of ceremonies. Child after child comes to offer firewood or trash for the blaze. Arthur, trudging home from work, pauses to watch. The blaze is ignited, and the traditional Fawkes dummy, in its pants and jacket, flares up. The clothing burns away. Arthur perceives the white limbs and the white face that ignites with a soft explosion —it is none other than his dummy, his Auntie Gracie!

Rage seizes him. Bent on revenge against Anthony, he goes home. There is a letter on the table. He remembers Anthony's telephoned words: "Your next letter is your last chance."

Arthur opens the letter. "I have played fast and loose with you long enough. I have chosen, Tony. I have chosen you. Say the word and I can be with you by Saturday. Say it, and I will run to you even if I have to run from Roger in my nightdress. I love you. H."

An eye for an eye, thinks Arthur. Anthony has taken his lady away. *He* will steal *Anthony*'s woman. He shoves the letter into his pocket, goes to his cellar. There is nothing there now but a heap of dirty clothes.

He goes out and the city receives him into its arteries. The pattern, twice before experienced, is repeating itself without his volition.

He waits in the Vale, and he sees the woman coming. He feels, smells, absorbs her terror as he wrenches off his tie, twists it around her neck. . . .

The next morning, the police knock on every door in the house. Everyone is to be questioned. The murder victim is Mrs. Vesta Kotowski; her husband, Brian, has disappeared.

Anthony is at the library, reading everything he can find about the Kenbourne Killer. Is the killer back in circulation again, after almost twenty years?

The police question Arthur about his whereabouts the previous evening and he tells them that he has been home all evening long. Even as they leave, he remembers. Anthony has seen him come in just before midnight. He will be able to tell the police that Arthur has lied.

Carefully, Arthur makes his plans.

The dark lusts that invade the prim bachelor, Arthur, unfold in that microcosm of metropolitan menace that Rendell has created in Kenbourne Vale, London. "Ruth Rendell-land" one reviewer called it, as the author conveys with unnerving accuracy the pervert who periodically strangles a department story dummy in the cellar until this strange safety valve is appropriated for a Guy Fawkes bonfire; the lover whose mail is intercepted, at first by accident, and then by design. (This tampering with vital correspondence the reader watches in a way that is almost painful.) Rendell performs her delicious balancing act skillfully as the various story lines are spun to their relentless and shocking conclusion.

Each character in a Rendell book is brilliantly realized; the atmosphere is true, and, in truth, there is little reason to dispute the judgment of the *Boston Globe* critic who points to Mrs. Rendell as the best mystery writer in the English-speaking world.

12

Dorothy Uhnak

The Mean Street Beat

"When I write a book, I know the beginning and the end. In between I build my case on the investigative methods a careful police officer uses, and the cases are a revelation to me," says Dorothy Uhnak of New York City. Uhnak's books are heavily peopled with the cops, con men and criminals she met during her years on the police force. "I was like a sponge when I was on the force, observing everything while I was a participant," said Uhnak in a recent interview in the *New York Times Review of Books.*[1] "It wasn't enough for me to have a case, wind it up and be finished with it."

Uhnak, a pretty blonde woman in her early fifties, grew up in and around New York City. She has one sister, is half Jewish and half Irish, and was born in the Bronx. She has been writing "ever since I can remember."

"There was poetry at five, followed by all the stages an unskilled writer follows. Verse, blank verse, free verse. Short stories, novellas, plays. No matter what else I've been doing in my life, I've been writing."

Uhnak attended the College of the City of New York for three years, dropped out to become a policewoman with the New York Transit Department.

"In those days, training was almost nonexistent. There was something of an emergency in the Transit Department, and they were anxious to get people out in the streets working; they didn't have the luxury of putting women in desk jobs to free men for patrol. We were right out there, in advance of other police departments. I was on patrol in the early fifties with a male partner.

"We learned by doing. The only thing the department was careful about was training in the use of weapons. I had a small, but adequate, Smith & Wesson, which I knew how to use.

"I was with the Transit Department for fourteen years, with time out only for the birth of my daughter, Tracy," Uhnak continued in a telephone interview with me during the winter of 1984. "But I wasn't allowed to take the examination for promotion, so after fourteen years, I left the department and returned to college, this time to the John Jay College of Criminal Justice."

Uhnak's first book, *Policewoman* (1964), was an autobiographical story, written at odd moments as she juggled career, marriage and motherhood. Her next three books were about Christie Opara, a young policewoman. The first of these—*The Bait* (1968)—won Uhnak the Edgar for Best First Novel of 1968. *The Investigation* (1977) is thought to be based on events in the case of Alice Crimmins, the cocktail-lounge waitress in Queens who was accused of murdering her two children.

"I'm concerned with New York City—its ethnic mix, its politics," said Uhnak to me. "Though fiction, my books deal in reality. My degree is in criminal justice—not English lit."

Uhnak has written eight books, is at work on her ninth.

"I've been fortunate. I've had the same publisher for twenty years—and I've worked with good editors. My first editor was Barbara Norville, who was one of the best. The first books—the Opara books—were genre books. Then in 1972 Michael Korda took over my career, with *Law and Order*. He's handled my books ever since. We have a sympatico relationship. He'll read what I've written, then send me a list of crucial questions—and by the time all the questions are answered to Michael's and my satisfaction I should have a book."

What was Uhnak's first big sale?

"Well, I never went from subsistence to big dollars. The Christie Opara trilogy came about when Robert Gottlieb, editor-in-chief at Simon & Schuster, showed *Reader's Digest* my first Opara book. The *Digest* bought it. I got thirty thousand dollars from that sale, and from the next book, as well. Then it was picked up for movies, then television—but that was a gradual building process."

"My first big take-your-breath-away sale was *Law and Order*, a book about several generations of policemen in New York. It was my *Roots*; I went back to the streets of my childhood to write it, and it's still my favorite book. Pocket Books bought it for $250,000 and two days later Paramount bought the film rights for $350,000. The accountant came over to the house, just looked at us and said '*Oh*, my *God*!'"

Uhnak is involved in the lean, muscular realism of crime, and she lets nothing in her past go to waste in her pursuit of this realism. "I brought everything home with me from my police force job. Once I arrested a character in the subway—a flasher—and through the years I'd go home and write endless short stories about him. He finally evolved as a rapist-murderer in my first novel.

"Over the years, the unpublished short stories—character sketches, really—have become useful to me. Now, when I'm searching for just the right character for a book or a situation I go back to these earlier writings. Nothing's ever wasted."

Uhnak's last book, *False Witness* (1981), explores questions of crime and justice as they revolve around two women: Sanderalee Dawson, a black television personality, and Lynne Jacobi, an assistant district attorney who needs a conviction in order to succeed her boss, running for the senate. The book was on the best-seller lists both as a hardcover novel and as a paperback in 1982–83. Between this book and Uhnak's work-in-progress was an ill-fated venture into television writing which "turned out to be a terrible waste of time and energy."

Daughter Tracy is now grown and living in her own apartment. The Uhnaks divide their time between Queens and a "white elephant" of a house on the water at Shelter Island that the entire family adores.

"My husband is an engineer, so when we bought the Shelter Island home eight years ago, he thought, 'this'll be easy.' Eight years later we are still working on it."

Despite Uhnak's denial of instant wealth from either *Law and Order* and *False Witness*, the money earned from her books has enabled her to do some comfortable things. "I support some animal charities." There are currently two dogs and five cats in residence Chez Uhnak. "I bought a condo for my parents and an apartment for my daughter. I have my own personal scholarships, with which I help privately some very bright people."

There is a certain irony that Uhnak's books, dealing in the grim and dusty reality of New York City crime as they do (and read admiringly in many station houses), have helped foster the tranquil fantasy life that the Uhnaks now enjoy on Shelter Island.

I spoke to Michael Korda, editor in chief of Simon & Schuster Publishing Company, and Uhnak's editor, about her.

"Dorothy was never a 'genre' writer. In the days before television's *Hill Street Blues*, even before there was a *Serpico* book or motion picture, along came this policewoman who wrote an excellent and, I think, rather sensational book—*Policewoman*. Then, her next book, the first one about Christie Opara—*The Bait*—was good, too. Her next two books about Christie also did well. At that point, we got rid of our mystery department and our mystery editor, and I said to Dorothy:

"'Look, you've got to stop doing these series books. It's pointless. You are too good. You do one thing until you learn your craft; but once you learn it you must go on to something else.'

"I became Dorothy's editor. I like working with her. She has developed her skills from book to book. She's become a phenomenally good writer. She is, in addition, a interesting, tough, *nice* woman.

"But I don't know if there is such a thing as the 'mystery' genre any more. Are Dorothy's books 'mysteries'? Call them by that name if you want to. I just know what books I think will work commercially and are fine books as well. Dorothy's succeed on both counts."

False Witness

"I write about the reality of crime," says Uhnak. One reality of crime in the United States is that it has become commonplace. No longer is murder the "unique crime" that P. D. James regards it. Murder is committed by children under fourteen, who spin through the revolving door of the juvenile justice system to kill again. Murder is committed by junkies in need of fixes. It is committed by members of a small group bound loosely together at a given time for socio-political or religious reasons, who aver that their killings are not murders but necessary steps in their marches to freedom. Murder is done by the mentally ill, and by the socially deprived.

What Uhnak does is to pull back from her fictional crime(s) and her criminal(s) and examine each, not under the monomaniacal magnifying glass focus of, say, a Conan Doyle or an Antonia Fraser, but through the panoramic lens of a wide-focus camera, catching a big-city crime that sends first shock waves, then small ripples from its victims' centers throughout the city around them.

False Witness is the story of a gruesome crime, and the way it changes the lives of the victim, the investigators, the criminal. At the center of the story are two very different women, each tough, ambitious, successful in her own way.

First, the victim. She is Sanderalee Dawson, a beautiful, black, famous, sexy, female television talk show hostess, controversial, enjoying her hard-won and hard-held celebrity, raped and savagely mutilated in her own apartment.

> She opened her eyes and gazed without understanding at the pendulum motion of the telephone receiver as it skimmed the floor, dangling from the end of the uncurled white rubberized cord.
>
> There was a hand holding the receiver, the fingers locked in a rigid grasp. It was a severed hand and a thick trail of blood followed the back and forth swaying motion, in a bright red pattern on her white ceramic tile kitchen floor. It was hers.

So begins the prologue of *False Witness*. The story is told by the second woman at the center of the story, Lynne Jacobi, bureau chief of the District Attorney's office, a brilliant, abrasive young woman who wants to be DA so badly she can almost taste it, and who finds the job within her grasp. Her DA boss has been picked to run for the senate, and he will pick Lynne as his replacement—if she can get a conviction for the crime.

Lynne is picked up by one of the assistant DAs, Bobby Jones, a handsome midwestern Wasp type, who has worked for Lynne for several years. They work well together; they are also lovers.

Together they go to the Fifty-seventh Street New York City

apartment where Sanderalee Dawson has just been taken to the hospital, barely alive. Timothy Doyle, the old doorman of the apartment building, admits them; he is visibly shaken. It was he who had taken Miss Dawson up to her apartment in her running clothes, along with a stranger, a white man, who was also dressed in running clothes; and it was Doyle who had gone up to the apartment when her phone was pulled off the hook, and who had found her, trailing her own blood, on the kitchen floor. Doyle tells Lynne and Bobby that Sanderalee came in from doing her television talk show about 1:30 A.M., went up to her eighth floor apartment and came down again about fifteen minutes later in her jogging clothes and blue angora hat and scarf, it being frigid outside. She ran off.

An hour later, Sanderalee returned, this time with a male jogger, a tall, white man—Doyle knows the man is white, but didn't see his face. "I didn't look at his face." Doyle, it seemed, was discreet. He took the two of them up to the eighth floor, and looked at their shoes the entire time. He remembered that there was something "funny" about the shoes of the unknown male jogger.

An hour later, the light on Doyle's switchboard flashed on from the girl's apartment "and the sounds coming from that poor girl's telephone made me run right out and flag a patrol car. Two young patrolmen came and I took them up in the elevator.

"At first we couldn't find her. We heard the noise, softly, groaning, like a wee animal. Then we went into the kitchen. Walked past all the upset in the living room, furniture turned over. And the blood. There she was, all broken and bleeding."

One patrolman tells the other to phone for an ambulance. Sanderalee's hand has been severed from her arm, and grips the phone. They remove the severed hand and put it in a bag of ice cubes.

"The one young policeman tried to help her breathe, giving her the kiss of life. Then he realized something was blocking her windpipe, and sucked it out and cleared her breathing apparatus."

It was her lip; the victim had bitten it off in her agony. She is bundled up and taken to the Hospital for Special Surgery, more dead than alive. Bobby and Lynne follow her to the hospital.

There chaos reigns, but they are accustomed to caring for the rich, the famous, the infamous, the exotic. They are, in a word, used to press conferences. The public relations man keeps the press posted;

surgery commences: a three-man surgical team noted for its work in the field of microsurgery are attempting to reattach Dawson's hand.

The television executives, Sanderalee's bosses, bemoan this happening during a "sweeps week." Notes one: "the ratings: down the toilet."

Lucy Capella, Lynne's investigator, also a lawyer and an ex-nun, is on hand and is detailed to stay in the hospital right by the victim, in case the victim says anything.

At her office the next morning, Lynne is summoned by her patrician boss, Jameson Whitney Hale, attractive and ambitious. He asks her about Sanderalee.

"I was the right person to ask. I had appeared several times on her talk show; furthermore, Sanderalee and I were born on the same day of the same year, within fifteen minutes of each other. We discovered this talking together after her show."

There the resemblance stops. Sanderalee is astonishing looking, the cocoa-colored skin, and delicate features, the cheekbones that catch the light and shadow in extraordinary ways. Black is indeed beautiful, thinks Lynne.

Lynne tells Whitney about Sanderalee's rise. First as a thin black waif, discovered by a French film director as he made his first Harlem motion picture featuring Sanderalee. She then became a model, and, finally, tiring of being a mannequin, starred in a television commercial. From there, she was given her own show, where her spice and her spunk made her immediately controversial.

Sanderalee has a new mentor: Dr. Regg Morris, a highly visible, vocal determined advocate of the aims, policies and methods of the PLO. Sanderalee had made a highly publicized trip to Arafatland, where she had been photographed with Arafat and his band.

Sanderalee's savvy, according to Lynne, was shallow. She was inclined to pick up on the wave length of any current guru (the one previous to Morris had been a black entertainer with gold chains, tight pants, and plenty of scorn for anyone or anything white; during his reign with Dawson there had been a self-consciously "black" attitude throughout her show). And Arafat?

She was indifferent to representatives of the government who tried in vain to explain to her the delicate mid-Eastern situation, the Camp David accords. One in particular; she listened to him briefly, turned her head away and finished her program by saying to him:

"You're a Jew aren't you?"

And when the man assented, Sanderalee looked into the camera and said:

"I rest my case."

Sanderalee had been getting away with this type of behavior for several years.

Hale talks to Lynne about getting herself better known, particularly if she wants to have his job when he resigns to run for the senate. What he has in mind is a television show by a woman, Glori Nichols, who wants to do a documentary about three successful women making it in the world of men; she would like to "do" Lynne, who doesn't think much of the idea.

Dr. David Cohen, head of the microsurgery team who has reattached Sanderalee's hand, is on television. He introduces his colleagues, Dr. Waverly and Dr. Esposito, talks to them briefly. He has, he says, no plans yet to begin the cosmetic surgery on Ms. Dawson's face.

Meanwhile Lucy Capella keeps watch at Sanderalee's bedside, in case the girl comes out of her coma. She is holding her own. Deep down in her coma, she is beginning to stir.

Bobby Jones takes Lynne to an all-night spot frequented by joggers, called Jog-On-In, where, they learn, Sanderalee is in the habit of stopping when she jogs after her show.

A photographer, Alan Greco, who has taken pictures of Sanderalee for *Vogue*, meets the two of them. A good friend of Sanderalee, he knows that, lately, she has often been totally indiscreet, picking up men when she jogged, taking them back to her apartment. He wants them to give his love to Sanderalee when she awakens.

Lynne goes to the hospital. Sanderalee is shuddering awake. She asks to see Regg Morris. He is brought to her bedside, where he is going to stay.

When Lynne returns to her office, Glori Nichols is there. Glori is so persistent and confident that it finally dawns on Lynne that there is something going on between her boss and Nichols. She realizes that Nichols will not let up until she gets what she wants: Lynne on film for her documentary.

From the hospital Lucy calls Lynne, telling her to get up there with a tape recorder as fast as she can. Lynne and Lucy go to Sanderalee's bedside, where the victim says she is now ready to make a statement.

She tells them that the night of her attack, she was running and turned her ankle. Another jogger came up to her and told her that he was a doctor and could fix her foot so that it wouldn't swell. She invited him up to her apartment, where he fixed her ankle, but then, as she turned to mix him a drink, he attacked her. It was a vicious unprincipled physical attack, after which he raped and sodomized her, then, when she attempted to phone for help, attacked her with the cleaver.

"Who did it, Sanderalee?" asks Lucy. "Who did these terrible things to you?"

"The tall one with the glasses. The surgeon who they told me did the most work reattaching my hand. He did this to me. It was Dr. David Cohen!"

There is chaos among Lynne's staff. Lucy and Lynne think that Cohen might have been guilty. Bobby finds it difficult to believe that a doctor would behave in such a way. Lynne and Bobby argue about it, but nevertheless they begin to do what they have to do: find out all they can about Dr. David Cohen.

The first thing that they find out about Dr. Cohen is that he is a long-time jogger. Second, that he was rejected for military service because of a disability. Third, the doctor is a widower; his wife died in a fall from the balcony of their penthouse apartment several years before.

Armed with the autopsy report on Melissa Cohen's death, Lynne visits the psychiatrist whom the late Mrs. Cohen saw regularly. The doctor tells Lynne about Mrs. Cohen's death. A manic depressive, she was at the beginning of a manic phase, raced through her apartment, leaned on her balcony, reached out her arms—and fell to her death.

From the doctor Lynne elicits that he was giving Mrs. Cohen the drug lithium; later he discovered that Mrs. Cohen was not manic depressive, only depressive—and thus was unlikely to have been racing around her apartment. When Dr. Cohen said that his wife was manic depressive, why didn't her psychiatrist correct him? It was something about grants—the psychiatrist was in the midst of asking for a large grant and couldn't risk muddying the waters.

And so Dr. Cohen lied to the police about his wife's death.

Lynne visits Mrs. Cohen's parents to find out that they've always felt their son-in-law David was schizophrenic; they thought that *he* killed their only daughter. As Lynne leaves, the parents whisper: "Get him! Oh, please, get him!"

Further digging locates the shoe company that makes jogging shoes for Dr. Cohen; due to a childhood bout with polio, one of his legs is shorter than the other. They made four pairs of shoes for the doctor. But a search of the doctor's office, apartment, and house in East Hampton turns up only three pairs. What has happened to the fourth?

Despite Bobby's reluctance to believe that the doctor can have done such a thing, Lynne arrests Dr. David Cohen for aggravated assault, rape, sodomy, and dismemberment.

On the day of the hearing the courtroom is packed. The defendant, stony-faced and defiant, is there beside his high-priced lawyer. Behind him sits his mother—stiff, arthritic, in a wheelchair—and his brother and father.

Before the proceedings begin, the doctor's father falls over with a heart attack and dies. His brother has an epileptic fit, and with the ruins of her family fallen around her the old woman looks up at Lynne and delivers a curse upon her head.

Uhnak's mix, dealing with ethnic New York, ethical New York, the politics of the district attorney's office, and the glittering city world of television, is a potent one—a sensation from page 1.

"What's interesting to me," Uhnak told me, "is that I wrote the book *before* Elizabeth Holtzman was elected district attorney of one of New York's counties. But the fact that a woman could be elected to that job was an indication that the timing was right for my book."

All of the questions raised during this "mix" of the lives and loves of two fascinating career women are answered finally before the end of the Uhnak book. All except one, and that one is left to the reader to puzzle out alone.

The book is a shocker, imposing its horrifying ordeal on the lives of its victims, the careers of the investigating team, and the love affair of the assistant district attorney and her chief investigator, Bobby Jones. But it is a shocker that millions of readers couldn't help reading.

13

Phyllis A. Whitney

Rebecca Redux

"Last night I dreamed I went to Manderley again."

So begins *Rebecca*, Daphne du Maurier's 1938 novel, with perhaps the most recognizable opening line in twentieth-century fiction. The story about a young heroine at the mercy of a strange older husband and a sinister servant owes much to the creations of the Brontë sisters—Charlotte's *Jane Eyre* and Emily's *Wuthering Heights*—and is the forerunner of today's popular novels of romantic suspense.

Undisputed successor to du Maurier in the field is Phyllis A. Whitney, who at eighty has sixty-eight books to her credit, including twenty-seven adult novels and thirty-three mysteries and novels for young adults. Whitney's *Thunder Heights* (1968), an Ace paperback, is considered the first of the modern paperback Gothics. "The editor at Ace Publishing Company saw his mother reading *Rebecca* and thought there might be a market for the same kind of books. That was the rebirth of the genre," says Whitney.

"The psychological interplay between a place and the characters who inhabit that place is what I write about," Whitney told me in a telephone interview. "I like to travel to a special island—or country or city—soak up its atmosphere and its traditions, and place my characters in that framework. I take snapshots of the place and any buildings I plan to write about, and then I go home to Long Island with my notes and my photographs and bring it all to life.

"Several years ago when I visited Palm Beach I was struck by the splendor of Mar-A-Lago, the estate of the late Marjorie Merriwether Post. From that outside glance I 'built' its interior for myself and 'furnished' it mentally for the book that became *Poinciana* (a book, incidentally, whose hardcover and paperback editions made the best-seller list of the *New York Times Book Review*).

"One of the crimes in the story was the theft of a priceless netsuke collection. I read all I could about netsukes, finding in my own library books about the subject I didn't even realize I owned, most of them from my childhood in the Orient."

Whitney, a small dynamo of a woman, with big eyes and long hair French-twisted up the back of her head, has traveled all over the world and used many of its historic sites and playgrounds as background for her books both for adults and young adults, although lately she has confined her travels to the United States.

She was born to American parents in Japan. The family moved to the Philippines when she was six and a short time later on to China. Whitney's full given name is Phyllis Ayame Whitney—"Ayame" is Japanese for "iris." When she was fifteen, her father, who was in the hotel business, died and she and her mother returned to the United States.

Her mother died before Whitney was seventeen. She then lived with an aunt in Chicago, where she graduated from high school when she was twenty years old.

"I had gone to missionary schools in the East and I was far behind American students academically," she said in an interview in the *New York Times* in January 1983.[1] "Finally I graduated and went to work in bookstores selling books. Later I worked as a book reviewer for the *Chicago Sun*. I couldn't go to college, but I did everything I could to educate myself.

"I had read young people's fiction in the old *St. Nicholas Magazine* and I began writing short stories in my teens. It was four years before I sold one to the *Chicago Daily News*. I wasn't very good, but I was very persistent. After that, it took me three years to sell three more stories."

Whitney married in 1925 and in 1931 gave birth to her only child. Two weeks after returning from the hospital with her new daughter, she began writing again. Working mothers, however, were a distinct minority in the thirties.

"I've always been liberated," pointed out Whitney. "After all, my background wasn't a traditional one."

Whitney said in the *Times* interview that in retrospect she thought her first marriage was a mistake, due in part to the fact that her husband was not supportive of her writing career. They divorced in 1944, by which time she was able to support herself and her daughter by writing and teaching writing classes.

Her first book, for young adults, was published in 1942: *A Place for Ann*. Her fourth, *Red Is for Murder*, was her first for adults. "I got about two thousand dollars for it, it sold nine hundred copies and I decided that writing for adults didn't pay, and I didn't write another adult novel for twelve years. After my name became well known, *Red Is for Murder* was brought out in paperback under the name *Red Carnelian*, where it did just fine.

"I'd written four books before I found a good writing teacher. I'm glad I didn't find a mentor too soon. Some professor might have gotten hold of me and my early efforts and said, 'Oh, no, no, no, no, no,' and I might have given up right there."

Finding the right creative writing teacher is all-important to a neophyte writer, Whitney feels. She has taught courses in writing at Northwestern University in Illinois and at New York University in New York City. Her *Guide to Good Fiction Writing*, published by The Writer, Inc., appeared in 1982.

"The most valuable advice I can give to a beginning writer is: 'Don't give up!' The test is: Do you want to write badly enough?

"There are a lot of people out there who say they want to become writers, but not many of them want to sit down and write. A writer *must* be willing to give up the time, to persist in writing."

At one time the Mystery Writers of America had an informal tutelage plan under which beginning writers, taking the regular course in mystery writing given by the organization, could ask the help of established writers, who are also members. A friend interested in writing mysteries for young adults once sent her manuscript to Whitney under this program.

"I can't tell you how generous and friendly and encouraging—and a lot of wonderful other things—Whitney was to me. She went over my manuscript, put notes on every page, and generally took reams of time with the book and with me," said the friend.

Whitney married again in 1950. Her husband was Lovell Jahnke, a Mobil Oil executive. "He was the right one." When Jahnke died in 1974, she moved from their hundred-acre estate in New Jersey to Brookhaven, New York, to be near her daughter.

Whitney keeps to strict work habits. "A lot of what I do is planning. After I've visited my 'place' I come home and work for two months in a notebook, fleshing out characters, working up a plot. I do a partial outline, working with my notes and my snapshots. I want to know who the villain is and where I'm going, but I don't want to know all the details. I want to surprise myself."

Much detailed firsthand research is at Whitney's fingertips in addition to the photographs she snaps of her current fictive site.

"When I go to a city—Palm Beach or Palm Springs—to research it as background for a book, I stop first at the Chamber of Commerce and get a city map. I need to be authentic; it wouldn't do to have my heroine driving her car south on a one-way northbound street."

Her habits of travel and work have enabled Whitney to produce almost a book a year. At Doubleday, where Whitney has been comfortably ensconced for many years, a separate "mainstream" editor handles the work of Whitney and other "blockbuster" writers such as Victoria Holt.

She also writes for softcover publishers. Her paperback *Thunder Heights* is generally considered the first modern romantic Gothic, its cover picturing the standard elements of a woman in white fleeing from a dark castle, a solitary light shining from the bell tower.

Whitney feels that women mystery writers generally aren't given the credit they deserve by the Mystery Writers of America. Her Edgars from this organization are all for her juvenile books and not for the books that make her a best-selling—and extremely wealthy—author.

"I wish I could think of a suitable name for the kind of writing I do," she wrote in a recent by-lined article in the 1981 *MWA Annual*. "We're read by millions of readers, yet we've never become quite—legitimate. 'Gothic' doesn't do it—too restrictive, and though I bow my helpless neck I think 'romantic suspense' sounds terribly sappy. Though we may have to accept that term for want of a better."

"Personally I hate categories," Whitney told me. "I consider myself an entertaining writer. My books have mystery, they have romance—but I don't want to be lumped with what passes for romance right now. My books are short on sex—explicit sex, that is. (*Jane Eyre* just throbs with sex, but it is never explicit.) I think you still might as well close the bedroom door. That may be old-fashioned, but my readers seem to like me." They do, indeed. *Vermilion* (1982), a recent success, was taken by the Literary Guild as a main selection as well as by the Reader's Digest Book Club.

Comparing the writing of the top women in the mystery field to the top men, Whitney says: "Our stories can be just as mystifying as those that the men write, but we usually get rid of detectives and police procedure as quickly as possible because we believe that sitting around adding up clues becomes boring and slows the action. We're very good at establishing moods and in making our backgrounds serve as characters in our stories. (Manderley was the heroine of *Rebecca*, not the first person writer—'I'—nor Rebecca herself.)"

To honor Whitney, The Patchogue-Medford Friends of the Library, near her Long Island home, recently sponsored a writing contest with awards of five hundred dollars apiece for the two winners. When one member suggested that perhaps she would rather have liked the funds to be applied to the purchase of a grand piano for library concerts, Whitney, overhearing the conversation, volunteered to buy the piano.

What does she do when she's between books, I asked her.

"I'm always writing a book. I may take a week off between novels, but I wouldn't know what to do with myself if I weren't working on some project or other. Books are at the base of my travels, and the places I visit wouldn't be as exciting to me if I weren't delving into their cultural, historical, geographical, and sociological aspects as background for a book. Take *Vermilion*. It has a fascinating background—Arizona, where three cultures (Anglo, Spanish, and Native American) coexist in a land of astonishing beauty, where deserts flow around mountains. I explored it in great depth and with great pleasure. I saw things there I'd never have seen if I hadn't been researching the background for my book.

"I recently returned from a trip to Hawaii. That's my 1987 book."

Two of Whitney's juveniles have won Edgars: *The Mystery of the Haunted Pool* (1960) and *The Mystery of the Hidden Hawk* (1963). She served as president of the Mystery Writers of America in 1975–76.

Poinciana

When Sharon Hollis marries Ross Logan it seems as if the nightmare of her recent past is over and her dreams are about to come true. Sharon's parents, internationally-known musical comedy star Ysobel Hollis, and her manager-husband, Ian, have been killed in a bomb blast in Northern Ireland. The blast has left Sharon wounded and in a hospital.

Ross Logan, once in love with Ysobel, rushes to Sharon's hospital bedside. A strong, intense man, the nearly sixty-year-old Ross is equally at home in London, Washington, or in Palm Beach, where his home, Poinciana, has been famous for its parties since the twenties. His mother, Allegra, was then doyenne of Palm Beach society.

Ross takes over in his masterful way. He reminds Sharon that he loved her parents too, and when she has recovered sufficiently, he carries her off to his London townhouse to recuperate. She grows stronger, and learns about Ross's family. He has been married twice. Helen, his first wife, died. Brett he divorced, but not before they had a daughter, Gretchen, now in her early twenties. Ross is worried about Vasily Karl, a Middle European of dubious background with whom Gretchen is running around.

Sharon is pressured by Ross to marry him. He wants to take her first to Japan for a combination business trip/honeymoon; after that they'll go to live at Poinciana.

Ross is a tender, gentle lover. Sharon relaxes, beginning to enjoy the world of the superrich into which she has married. One of its pleasures are the beautiful netsukes, carved figures of ivory, wood, and jade made by Oriental artists. Ross, a collector of the figures, buys Sharon a lovely one.

Their peaceful honeymoon is shattered by a long-distance phone call from Jarrett Nichols, Ross's executive assistant at Poinciana. Gretchen has married Vasily Karl and the two have moved into

Poinciana. Exasperated, the honeymoon ruined, Ross bundles Sharon into their jet, and they fly to Palm Beach.

Poinciana is a mansion in old Florida style, with a red tile roof, pale stucco frame, and a huge tower called the belvedere running up through the center of the building. It is a regal home, perfectly run by Mrs. Broderick, the housekeeper. Sharon is awed by the floors of white, lightly veined marble, the walls covered in tapestried silk. Stairs float upward to the second floor. Above the landing is a portrait by Sargent of the fabled Allegra. Poinciana itself seems like a grande dame: elegant, if a trifle seedy. Ross assures Sharon that what it needs is a woman's sure touch.

Sharon meets Jarrett Nichols, a red-haired man dressed in casual jeans and shetland sweater, whose office is in Poinciana, but who lives with his son—his wife is dead—in a small cottage on the estate's grounds, one of several such buildings.

Mrs. Broderick shows Sharon to her room. They pass the stairs leading up to the belvedere, which Mrs. Broderick says has a tower room overlooking the ocean. When Sharon asks the housekeeper what happened to Allegra, Mrs. Broderick suggests she "ask Mr. Logan." She points out Ross's bedroom next door to Sharon's room.

On her own, Sharon explores the house, discovers a beautiful ballroom and as she waltzes by herself, she is discovered by one of Poinciana's security men. She abruptly realizes what it will be like living in a museum.

On her way back to her room, Sharon runs into a curly redheaded boy playing with his dog: these are Jarrett's son and Brewster.

As Sharon dresses for dinner, Myra Ritter, about thirty-eight and Ross's secretary, comes to the bedroom to introduce herself to Sharon. The secretary's voice is faintly Germanic and she and Sharon talk about schools in Switzerland.

Before dinner, Sharon, wearing her netsuke, goes to the tower room. On its table she finds a group of very good photographs of Ross. As she looks at them, Gretchen comes in. It is she who has taken the photographs. She asks Sharon lightly which one of the pictures seems most like Ross. One is pensive, thoughtful; another is dynamic, charged with emotion. The pictures have been put out because a gallery is going to have an exhibition of Gretchen's work. Through the photographs the reader meets some of Poinciana's inhabitants. (One is of Pamela Nichols, killed in a car accident.) Vasily rushes in, and he and Gretchen fall into each other's arms – Sharon discovers that the dramatic encounter is the end of a lovers' quarrel.

Dinner is a stilted affair, filled with subtle tensions. Sharon shows off her netsuke, and Ross tells her that it is too valuable to wear, that the next day it will be taken to the netsuke room, where a place will be found for it to be displayed. Sharon is shocked. She felt the netsuke, which depicted a mother and child frog, was her own. After dinner, Ross and Sharon go upstairs. As Sharon is undressing, preparatory to going to Ross's room, she hears the sound of a record: it is "Blue Champagne," sung by her mother, Ysobel. She goes to Ross's bed, where he proceeds to make love to her with a strange, inspired passion. As he falls into a deep, satisfied sleep, Sharon has to accept the fact that he has poured out his love for Ysobel through Ysobel's daughter.

Ross takes Sharon to the netsuke room and asks her to catalog its treasures. The carvings are brightly colored, placed against backgrounds of mossy green and hollyhock red. She again asks Ross about his mother, and he finally takes her angrily to a window and points to one of the smaller cottages. He tells her that Allegra, now in her nineties and senile, lives there with a nurse.

Finally, Sharon asks Gretchen why Allegra has been banned from her own home and is living in a small cottage. Gretchen, who loves her grandmother, tells Sharon that Allegra tried to kill Ross one night.

Extremely upset, Sharon has her dinner tray brought to her bedroom, and later wanders about the grounds of Poinciana. Returning to the house, she uses the ballroom as a shortcut to her own loggia. As she mounts the steps to the second floor, she is pushed viciously by someone who whispers, "Go! Go away or you'll be sorry!"

She falls back, hitting her head on the marble floor. Dazed, she makes her way to her room, and is helped by Myra Ritter, whom she meets in the corridor. Myra calls Jarrett, who brings one of the guards with him. Jarrett calls Ross, on a visit to Palm Beach, who is very angry and who comes home.

Sharon goes to sleep, alone.

Next day she goes to the cottage where Allegra is making out lists for parties she will never again give. "The John Pillsburys of course, and Mrs. William Randolph Hearst. And the Huttons." Sharon introduces herself to Allegra. The two find themselves liking each other, though Allegra tends to fade in and out of conversations. Allegra loves her granddaughter, Gretchen; hates and fears her son, Ross.

Sharon makes her way to Jarrett's office. She has many questions, wants to become a friend to the intense, wiry Jarrett, who actually runs Ross's many diversified business interests. (She has discovered that it was Allegra who had plucked Jarrett from law school to assist Ross.)

Sharon goes to bed. Ross isn't in the room next door. She drops off to sleep and is awakened by an alarm bell. She rolls out of bed, runs next door to Ross's room. His bed has not been slept in. She runs downstairs to Ross's office, and there she discovers Ross slumped over his desk, fully dressed. Jarrett is there with him.

"I just found him," he tells the horrified Sharon. "I'm afraid he's gone. Heart, I think."

Jarrett calls the doctor and the police. Gretchen comes in. Jarrett explains that Ross, sounding upset, phoned him to come to the office. Has Gretchen done anything to upset him?

Gretchen, hysterical, shakes her head, but points her finger at Sharon, crying that Ross has had nothing but pain and disappointment since his marriage to her. In Ross's office Sharon finds a sheet of notepaper. Back in her room she reads it.

> Dad: If you send Vasily away, I will tell Jarrett what I know about you and Pam.

That is clear enough. Ross read the note and suffered the heart attack that killed him. Jarrett comes to Sharon's room and asks her to burn the note.

Next day, the house is in chaos. Allegra asserts herself and demands to be moved back in. Sharon is happy; she loves the old lady. Mrs. Broderick, the housekeeper, is not. "The old lady is sick."

Sharon knows that she is in for a rough time. Gretchen announces that she and Vasily plan to stay. Sharon must leave.

Next day as Sharon walks around the grounds of Poinciana, a scream from the direction of the base of the belvedere interrupts her stroll. She runs to the tower and finds the body of Gretchen sprawled on the ground. She rolls over the sad, broken body, now dead. A small figure rolls from Gretchen's hand. It is a netsuke, a carving of the Sleeping Mermaid, a favorite of Allegra's. The police close in on Sharon, Vasily, and Jarrett.

Every story has a setting. When setting is integrated into plot it becomes background. When setting affects actions and emotions of the characters, it becomes atmosphere. When setting becomes more important than characters, however, what you are left with is a diminution of story, because nothing is quite so interesting as people.

Whitney, then, is not entirely accurate when she says that "the heroine of *Rebecca* is Manderley." Fascinating characters, deftly limned, people the grounds and the rooms that are Manderley, three-dimensional characters that make you laugh, cry, tremble in anticipation, and swell with joyous love. They are satisfying people to know, people with whom you like to renew acquaintance periodically.

Such is not true of the people who dwell in Poinciana. One may care about the building, but one never gets to know more than two dimensions of the people who inhabit it. Whitney's stories generally include a dark secret that harks back a generation or two, but the fact that the people to whom the secret happened close ranks and go on living as if nothing shattering has occurred is simply not the way that real people behave.

So what you have in Whitney's books, then, is an agreeable story interwoven with a travelogue, or an architectural exploration, and the psychological profile of an interesting "place," peopled with rather two-dimensional characters, and a puzzle that Whitney hopes is unsolvable until the last page.

"I'm not very blood-thirsty," Whitney told me during a telephone interview. "I like to tantalize. I love intrigue and I love to fool my readers."

Readers so tantalized, intrigued and fooled, then, number in the millions; they have made Whitney an extremely wealthy woman. Her books, both hardcover and paperback, satisfy a large audience of faithful addicts.

Some critics of the author's chosen genre—romantic suspense—insist that it is formula writing without serious literary value. To which Whitney replies: "I don't care about critics. My goal is to write a better book each time. I simply try to tell a good story about interesting people." Usually she does that. To wish that she would go a little farther, dig a little deeper, is perhaps pointless.

Notes

2. Amanda Cross

1. Carolyn Heilbrun, review of *End Game*, by Michael Gilbert, *New York Times Book Review*, September 12, 1982.
2. Jean H. White, review of *Death in a Tenured Position*, by Amanda Cross, *Washington Post Book Review*, March 15, 1981.
3. Heilbrun, review of *A Coat of Varnish*, by C. P. Snow, *Washington Post Book Review*, November 18, 1979.

3. Dorothy Salisbury Davis

1. Quoted by Burroughs Mitchell in *The Education of an Editor* (Garden City, New York: Doubleday & Company, 1980) 87.
2. Quoted in 2-part interview, *Ellery Queen's Mystery Magazine*, January, February, 1984.
3. Ibid.
4. Ibid.
5. Ibid.
6. Ibid.
7. Quoted by Louis Kannenstine in *World Authors 1950–1970* (New York: H. W. Wilson, 1975) 363.

4. Lady Antonia Fraser

1. Jessica Mann, review of *Splash of Red*, by Lady Antonia Fraser, *Times Literary Supplement* (London), June 5, 1981.
2. Quoted in "Jemima Shore: Telly Detective," *Murderess Ink*, ed. Dilys Wynn (New York: Workman Publishing Company, 1979) 288–89.
3. Mann, op. cit.

5. Lucy Freeman

1. Quoted in "The Whydunit Emerges, Thanks to Freud," *The Murder Mystique*, ed. Lucy Freeman (New York: Frederick Ungar Publishing Co., 1982) 46.

6. Dorothy B. Hughes

1. Dorothy B. Hughes, letter to author, March, 1984.
2. Quoted in "Dorothy B. Hughes," *Encyclopedia of Mystery & Detection*, ed. Otto Penzler and Christopher Steinbrunner (New York: McGraw-Hill, 1976) 217.
3. Hughes, letter cited.
4. Otto Penzler and Christopher Steinbrunner, "Dorothy B. Hughes," *Encyclopedia of Mystery & Detection*, 218.

7. P. D. James

1. Gillian Freeman, review of *Deadlier Than the Male*, by Jessica Mann, *Times Literary Supplement* (London), June 5, 1981.
2. Quoted by Patricia Craig, interview of P. D. James, *London Sunday Times*, June 5, 1981.
3. Quoted by Craig.
4. Quoted by Mary Cantwell, Associated Press, November 14, 1982.

8. Emma Lathen

1. C. P. Snow, "Emma Lathen," *Financial Times* (London), May, 1970.
2. Max Hall, "The Case of the Wall Street Mysteries," *Harvard Magazine*, 1975.

3. Ibid.
4. Unsigned review of *Murder to Go*, *New Yorker Magazine*, February 21, 1970.
5. Quoted by John C. Carr in *The Craft of Crime* (Boston: Houghton Mifflin, 1983) 176.

9. Margaret Millar

1. Dilys Winn, *Murderess Ink* (New York: Workman Publishing Co., 1979) 78–79.

10. Shannon OCork

1. Newgate Callendar, review of *Sports Freak*, by Shannon OCork, *New York Times Book Review*, April 27, 1980.
2. Quoted in "The Truth, More or Less, as Long as It Makes a Good Story," *The Murder Mystique*, ed. Lucy Freeman (New York: Frederick Ungar Publishing Co., 1982) 137.
3. B. J. R. Stolper, article in *Scholastic*, October 22, 1938, quoted by Howard Haycraft in *Murder for Pleasure* (New York: Appleton & Co., 1941) 241.

11. Ruth Rendell

1. Francis Wyndnam, review of *Put on by Cunning*, by Ruth Rendell, *Times Literary Supplement* (London), June 5, 1981.
2. William A. Henry III, *Boston Sunday Globe*, November 1, 1981.
3. Dilys Winn, op. cit.

12. Dorothy Uhnak

1. Quoted by Edwin McDowell, *New York Times Review of Books*, October 25, 1981.

13. Phyllis A. Whitney

1. Quoted by Diana Greenberg, "Phyllis Whitney's Continuing Saga," *New York Times* (Long Island Section), January 2, 1983.

Selected Bibliography

Mary Higgins Clark

Where Are the Children? New York: Simon & Schuster, 1975
A Stranger Is Watching. New York: Simon & Schuster, 1977
The Cradle Will Fall. New York: Simon & Schuster, 1980
Stillwatch. New York: Simon & Schuster, 1984
(soft cover volumes, Dell Publishing Co, New York.)

Amanda Cross

The James Joyce Murder. New York: MacMillan, 1967
In the Last Analysis. New York: MacMillan, 1964
(soft cover publication, Avon Books, New York)
Poetic Justice. New York: Alfred Knopf, 1970
Death in a Tenured Position. New York: E. P. Dutton, 1981
Sweet Death, Kind Death. New York: E. P. Dutton, 1984

Dorothy Salisbury Davis

A Gentle Murderer. New York: Scribner, 1953
Where the Dark Streets Go. New York: Scribner, 1969
A Death in the Life. New York: Scribner, 1976
Scarlet Night. New York: Scribner, 1980
Lullaby of Murder. New York: Scribner, 1984

ANTONIA FRASER

Quiet as a Nun. New York: Viking, 1977
The Wild Island. New York: W. W. Norton, 1978
A Splash of Red. New York: W. W. Norton, 1981
Cool Repentance. New York: W. W. Norton, 1982

LUCY FREEMAN

Nonfiction

Before I Kill More. New York: Crown Publishing Co., 1955
The Story of Anna O. New York: Walker Publishing Co., 1972
Freud & Women. New York: Frederick Ungar Publishing, 1981
A Woman for All Seasons. New York: Beaufort Press, 1985

Fiction

The Dream. New York: Arbor House, 1971
The Psychiatrist Says Murder. New York: Arbor House, 1973
The Case on Cloud Nine. New York: Arbor House, 1975

DOROTHY B. HUGHES

The So Blue Marble. New York: Duell, Sloan & Pearce, 1940
The Fallen Sparrow. New York: Duell, Sloan & Pearce, 1942 (paperback edition: New York, Bantam Books, 1979)
In a Lonely Place. New York: Duell, Sloan & Pearce, 1947
The Davidian Report. New York: Duell, Sloan & Pearce, 1952
The Expendable Man. New York: Random House, 1963

P. D. JAMES

Cover Her Face. New York: Scribner, 1962
Shroud for a Nightingale. New York: Scribner, 1971
Death of an Expert Witness. New York: Scribner, 1977
Innocent Blood. New York: Scribner, 1980
The Skull Beneath the Skin. New York: Scribner, 1982

EMMA LATHEN

Murder against the Grain. New York: MacMillan, 1967
(Pocketbook Edition, New York, 1975)
A Stitch in Time. New York: Simon & Schuster, 1968
Green Grow the Dollars. New York: Simon & Schuster, 1982

MARGARET MILLAR

Beast in View. New York: Random House, 1955
(Paperback edition, New York, Avon Books, 1974; International Polygonics, 1983)
Beyond This Point Are Monsters. New York: Random House, 1970
The Murder of Miranda. New York: Random House, 1979

SHANNON OCORK

Sports Freak. New York: St. Martin's Press, 1980
End of the Line. New York: St. Martin's Press, 1981
Hell Bent for Heaven. New York: St. Martin's Press, 1983

RUTH RENDELL

The Face of Trespass. New York: Doubleday, 1974
A Judgement in Stone. New York: Doubleday, 1978
Make Death Love Me. New York: Doubleday, 1979
The Fever Tree (short story collection). New York: Pantheon, 1982
Death Notes. New York: Pantheon, New York, 1981

DOROTHY UHNAK

The Bait. New York: Simon & Schuster, 1968
(Edgar Winner for Best First Novel)
Law and Order. New York: Simon & Schuster, 1973
False Witness. New York: Simon & Schuster, 1981

Phyllis A. Whitney

Juvenile Mysteries

Mystery of the Haunted Pool. New York: Doubleday & Co., 1960 (Edgar Winner, Juvenile Category)
Secret of the Emerald Star. New York: Doubleday & Co., 1964 (Edgar Winner, Juvenile Category)

Romantic Suspense Fiction

Vermilion. New York: Doubleday & Company, 1981
Emerald. New York: Doubleday & Company, 1983
The Stone Bull. New York: Doubleday & Company, 1977
Poinciana. New York: Doubleday & Company, 1980
Dream of Orchids. New York: Doubleday & Company, 1985 (Ballantine Books, New York publishes Phyllis Whitney's paperback editions.)